Worshiping Heart

Key to a Relationship With God

CARROL JOHNSON SHEWMAKE

REVIEW AND HERALD® PUBLISHING ASSOCIATION
HAGERSTOWN, MD 21740

This book was
Edited by Gerald Wheeler
Copyedited by William Cleveland and James Cavil
Designed by Patricia S. Wegh
Cover illustration by Renata Roberts
Typeset: 11/13 Berkeley Book

PRINTED IN U.S.A.

02 01 00 99 98   5 4 3 2 1

R&H Cataloging Service
Shewmake, Carrol Johnson, 1927-

    The worshiping heart: key to a
relationship with God.

    1. Worship.   I. Title.

            248.3

ISBN 0-8280-1297-0

Contents

$\mathscr{I}ntroduction$

A little more than a year ago I received a letter from a pastor in Norway who had read my book *Sensing His Presence, Hearing His Voice* with "great joy." Now he wondered if I would be willing to come to his country and share that joy with the people in Norway.

I read the letter with amazement. Although I have traveled quite a bit throughout the United States to speak, I had never been to Europe and did not even possess a passport. The only foreign countries I had visited were Mexico and an occasional visit to Canada to attend Johnson family reunions at Hope Adventist Camp in British Columbia. Even more important, I had never spoken through an interpreter.

The pastor went on to say that in the past few years a number of speakers from the United States had come to Norway, and now he wondered if he could add my name to that list. In numbness I read his list of speakers: Hans LaRondelle, George Knight, Martin Weber, and Marvin Moore. Surely my name didn't belong on that list! In shock I looked up at my husband, who was reading the letter over my shoulder.

"Of course, I'm not going," I said.

"Why not?" he asked in surprise.

"Why not?" I echoed. "Honey, there are so many reasons! Read that list of persons he has had speak in his church. They are all well-known theologians or pastors. And they are all *men*. How could I compete with them?"

"You don't need to compete," my husband answered. "This pastor has read your book and liked your message. All you have to do is present what the Lord has given you."

"They speak Norwegian," I countered. "I have never spoken through an interpreter."

"So?" my husband asked. "There is always a first time."

"The plane fare would be too much. Of course, I can't go," I stated flatly.

My husband laughed. "You haven't even finished reading the letter. They will pay your fare, of course."

Sheepishly I read the rest of the letter. Yes, they would cover my fare and take care of my expenses while I was in Norway. I was left without excuses!

In retrospect I understand that my protests came because of my fears. Deep inside I was excited and pleased to have an opportunity to go to Norway. But I needed a lot of affirmation from my husband and first son, who lives with us, that it was really a feasible trip for a woman to make alone. They encouraged me all the way.

When I finally made the decision to go I became excited and could talk of nothing else!

Two weeks later I attended the fiftieth reunion of my La Sierra Academy graduation. What an exciting time we all had renewing friendships with classmates, many of whom I hadn't seen in 50 years.

As I stood in a small group after the potluck dinner I mentioned my invitation to speak in Norway. The husband of one of my classmates began looking at me strangely. Finally he asked, "What are you going to speak about?"

"Why, prayer," I answered quickly, going on with a conversation with a classmate.

I felt the eyes of the man still upon me, so I turned toward him again.

Introduction

"What can you possibly tell the people of Norway about prayer that their own pastors can't tell them?" he inquired.

My eyes widened as I considered his question. *Yes, I wondered in sudden consternation, why was I going to Norway? What did I have to say?*

Immediately the Holy Spirit spoke to my heart.

"No one can tell my story," I told the man. "Each person has an individual experience with the Lord. My personal experience in prayer is what I can share that no one else can."

This is all I ever seek to do. Either in books or in speaking, I tell the story of what God has been and is doing in my life. Of course, I must always remember that my experience can never be depended upon to guide even me, much less others. Scripture is our only safe guide, and we must always interpret our experiences by the Bible. God never works in a way contrary to Bible truth. But developing an intimacy with God in my own personal experience gives me the courage to step out in writing and speaking, knowing that as I trust Him to guide me, my words will be for His honor and glory.

When I was born again in my teens I knew I had found my heart's desire. For weeks I walked in joy and contentment in Christ. But often the close sense of His presence faded as life's activities increased. Continually I deliberately had to rekindle my first love. Time and time again God opened up to me new vistas of His plans for my daily relationship with Him.

God has given me one all-consuming theme: *that He desires to have an intimate family relationship with each of us.* The Lord has led me to explore this topic extensively, to experience it for myself, and then to share my findings with others.

I have shared my personal story—step by step—in *Practical Pointers to Personal Prayer; Sanctuary Secrets to Personal Prayer; Sensing His Presence, Hearing His Voice;* and *When We Pray for Others.* But there is still another dimension to intimacy with God that I have scarcely touched upon—not what I can *get* from God (answers to prayers, blessings, a sense of His presence, etc.), but what I can *give* to Him: worship.

In this book I am telling my worship story, not yours. But hopefully my story will touch a response in your heart.

PROLOGUE

Spectacular Double Feature

The Three stood together, gazing around them at a world alive with movement, sound, and color. Where only days before had been darkness and emptiness, now mountains and valleys, rivers and lakes, trees and vegetation of all kinds flourished. Birds, fish, land animals, and water mammals cavorted in their native elements. Sunlight sparkled off the water like jewels and highlighted the peaks, accenting the riotous colors of a brand-new world.

"Oh, it's so good!" exclaimed the Son.

"Very good," agreed the Father.

"Perfect, as usual," the Spirit breathed.

Angels, reveling in the beauty of this new world, shouted in holy joy. "Hallelujah," they chorused. "Look what God has done! Praise Him, praise Him! Who else but God could have done this? Holy, holy, holy is the Lord God!"

The Holy Three smiled in perfect unity and anticipation.

"It's all ready," the Father said.

"Just waiting," the Spirit added eagerly.

"One more thing will make this world complete," commented the Son. And then He spoke clearly and authoritatively into the pure air of a brand-new planet: "Let us make man in our image."

God the Son spoke for all Three. The apostle John, who lived and worked with the Son when He became a man, described Jesus, the Son of God, as "the Word." By the word of the Son everything created came into being out of nothing except the power of that Word.

The Bible tells us that God formed all living creatures from the dust of the ground. But with humanity God showed His special involvement. After forming a male body out of the clay of the earth with His own divine hands, God the Son breathed into the completed figure the breath of life and lifted him to walk upright—a being created in the image of the God who formed him. "So God created man in his own image, in the image of God, he created him; male and female he created them" (Gen. 1:27).

The Three smiled upon the man! And upon the woman whom God created in the same intimate hands-on way—but this time beginning His creation with a rib taken from the man to symbolize that the two, male and female, were two parts of a perfect whole. Talk about good—this was the best! Earth's creation was now complete. The angels marveled, then burst into a new song of praise.

No human eye viewed the act of Creation. Adam and Eve came into the event well along toward its close. Besides, their eyes, newly formed, centered on God Himself, and they had no idea of the extravagance of the entire spectacle. Even if the first couple were available today to answer our questions, they would not have all the answers. The writer of the book of Genesis, under the Holy Spirit's instruction, gives us only a bare-bones description of this astounding event. Could it be that God is asking each of us to stretch our minds in imagination right from the very time we first read the Creation story—to become personally involved, so to speak—in order to reach out and worship Him? Any detail we add beyond the Genesis account can be only conjecture on our part—our imaginations at play with holy events. The only reason I have for toying with details of Creation is to cause my mind to view the creation of our earth from a new angle, to seek to help my mind recognize the absolute reality of God's act of creating our world and then fashioning a human being—awesome, wondrous, impossible for any being other than God.

Often I've read the biblical account so routinely that my mind tends to slide over the details and ceases to stand in awe of the act of Creation. But until I renew that awe I cannot truly worship God. For Creation *established* God's claim to Lordship and worship.

One more event affected the inhabitants of our world even more profoundly than Creation. God Himself came to live with us to repair the breach caused by sin. The Bible records the 33 years of His holy human life in much more detail than the account of Creation. His death and resurrection *doubled* His claim to worship. Contemplating this extraordinary transaction—His life for ours—creates in us what the Bible calls *fear of the Lord,* a sense of our creatureship: awe, respect, and obedient love. We view Him with adoration and love.

CHAPTER 1

What Can I Give God?

Every morning God calls me to commune with Him and to bring something with me. But it is not my offering, not even just my need. He desires my worship.

God created humanity in His own image, different from the animals in that He gave human beings an intelligent mind able to reason. And in that mind God planted the need and desire to worship a higher power intelligently. Even though Adam and Eve's sin broke off their face-to-face relationship with God, it did not eliminate their desire and need to worship. All through both biblical and secular history we see the results of this need in all humankind: those who follow Adam and Eve in repentance worship the Creator-God, while those who reject Him create their own gods. All humanity craves to worship.

In my other books I have talked about personal prayer, a sense of God's presence in daily living, and the ministry of intercession that He gives us. But no relationship with God can be complete without worship: the yearning of the inmost being of a man or woman after God in recognition that we are created beings and dependent upon the One who designed us. Since Adam's sin this reaching out begins not at our physical birth, but at the new birth, when the soul first surrenders completely to God. But few of us dip deep into the area of worship. Sadly, it is not a daily experience for most believers. But for us to mature as Christians and be ready for translation we must learn to choose that experience daily.

One of the reasons we seldom reach that far inward is that it is a rather scary business. Honesty—an integral part of worship—is awesome. Most of us have safely fashioned our lives by building up a facade. How can we face the depths of what we are in contrast to the greatness and majesty of God, our Creator? We will have to let go of all the defenses we have built up to protect ourselves from seeing ourselves as we really are. And in the process of discarding them we may find ourselves unmasked before the world also.

But we will have to be willing to shed the pride that hides our insufficiencies and accept the incredible fact that despite our unattractiveness and awkwardness God loves us and can use us in His service—not because we are so talented and clever, but because He can change and empower us by the Holy Spirit. And we will have to be willing to be obedient in every part of our lives, holding nothing back. The Bible and early Adventist Church history tell some almost unbelievable stories about what has happened when the creature was willing to become vulnerable in worship before the Creator. Pentecost was surely beyond the control of human beings! Dare we take that risk?

The Holy Spirit is the member of the Godhead most actively involved in worship. Until Jesus came to earth, God's people understood the Holy Spirit mainly as a power or influence emanating from God. But just before Jesus died on the cross He tried to explain to His disciples the vital role of the Holy Spirit, as the third person of the Godhead, in the lives of human beings.

"There's so much I want to tell you," Jesus told His closest friends, "but you can't understand it now. After I am gone I am going to send to you another member of the Godhead, the Spirit of truth, the Counselor, and He will be able to take the things I have longed to tell you and guide you into understanding truth" (paraphrase of John 16:12-15). After Jesus ascended into heaven, the Holy Spirit would take His place as guide and instructor for the disciples.

We humans are so deaf when it comes to spiritual things. But the Holy Spirit, in His quiet, penetrating way, can get our attention despite the loudest clamor. And as He speaks and we begin to understand, we will bring glory to God by our whole-hearted worship.

Human words are inadequate to explain spiritual truths. That is why we find Bible writers using different words to explain the same things. Jesus said, "I am the bread of life" (John 6:35); "I am the good shepherd" (John 10:11, 14); "I am the gate for the sheep" (verse 7); "I am the resurrection and the life" (John 11:25); "I am the light of the world" (John 8:12); and "I am the true vine" (John 15:1). None of these things in themselves are alike. Yet combined with Holy Spirit illumination, they add up to build a picture of God that we could get in no other way. We cannot *wholly* picture God either in mind or in words. We will always have more to understand. But God encourages us to study Scripture, meditate, and purposefully dig deeper into understanding so as to worship Him with greater faith, reaching beyond human logic or intelligence. *Read to*

Years of formal education or the degree of social or economic status that we have achieved do not necessarily prepare us to worship God. Children may have at least one advantage in worship in their willing response to the call of the Holy Spirit, because the only way to please God is to exhibit the childlike traits of openness, honesty, and obedience.

When Jesus met the woman at the well in Samaria, they discussed worship. Although despised even by her own people, she discovered, to her surprise, that a Jewish Man was willing to talk to her about such a mundane thing as a drink of water. "For," the Bible writer succinctly states, "Jews do not associate with Samaritans" (John 4:9). Much less *a Jewish man* with *a Samaritan woman!*

As the conversation progressed, Jesus led her from thinking about the water in the Samaritan well to spiritual water that could heal her rejected heart and quench her thirsting soul. As

He pried open her intimate secrets, she stared in shock. Perhaps she was only trying to take the attention from herself when she introduced the subject of worship.

"'Sir,' the woman said, 'I can see that you are a prophet. Our fathers worshiped on this mountain, but you Jews claim that the place where we must worship is in Jerusalem.'

"Jesus declared, 'Believe me, woman, a time is coming when you will worship the Father neither on this mountain nor in Jerusalem. You Samaritans worship what you do not know, we worship what we do know, for salvation is from the Jews. Yet a time is coming and has now come when the true worshipers will worship the Father in spirit and truth, for they are the kind of worshipers the Father seeks. God is spirit, and His worshipers must worship in spirit and in truth'" (John 4:19-24).

Jesus talks here about three kinds of worship: the worship of the Samaritans, which was mixed with idolatry; the worship of the Jews, which focused on the directions Moses had given them; and the spiritual worship that Jesus came to reveal. It is this third worship that is the theme of this book. Jesus pointed out that it is not important whether we worship on this mountain or at Jerusalem—it is not the place we worship, or the structure of the worship service, or the forms we use in prayer—but the spiritual uplifting of the creature's heart to the Creator in humility and contrition, in "spirit and in truth."

And how can we possibly do this in our flawed condition? It is often as though a locked door blocks us from heaven. How can we find the key to open it so that we may worship in spirit and in truth?

One day when my children were very small I was riding beside my husband in the car, the back seat filled with children— just an ordinary day. But as I chanced to look up at the beautiful blue sky and the floating clouds, I caught my breath. Suddenly I realized the proximity of heaven. There beyond the clouds I could imagine a door opening into God's presence. It was as though that door were slightly ajar. With all my heart I wanted to push it wide open and gaze into heaven. An intense longing filled me as I realized that I knew little of how to worship God.

From then on I looked for the door. But it was years before I discovered the key that would unlock it so that I could begin to understand the foundation of worship.

We might discover the key to worship in many different ways. We are all different, coming from different cultures, personalities, and lifestyles. Each of us has unique parents, heritage, and education. The wonderful thing about God is His ability and willingness to deal with each of us in our own individuality. (I'm only telling my story, not yours. But I think you will find some similarities between my experience and yours.)

Through the years it would sometimes seem that the door mysteriously stood wide open, and during that time I would eagerly immerse myself in worship. But then it would suddenly slam shut in my face. I always assumed that once I found the key, the door would swing open again and again.

You may think I am talking in riddles, but I don't know a better way to explain my intense search for meaningful worship. I do not mean to imply that God is deliberately making it hard for us to worship, or that *He* slammed the door shut in my face. Rather I want to illustrate the difficulty the fallen creature finds in yielding submission to the Creator in worship, asking for nothing, giving all.

Summary

Each morning God calls us to spend time in intimate communion with Him as we offer Him our worship. At Creation God planted in the minds of Adam and Eve the desire to intelligently worship a higher power. Even sin did not eliminate that drive in humanity. Those who have chosen the Creator God worship Him, while those who reject Him create their own gods.

No relationship with God is complete without worship. Worship is the yearning of the inmost being of a man or woman after God, a recognition that we are created beings and dependent upon the One who designed us. Our reaching for God begins when we first surrender completely to God at the new birth. But unfortunately, we seldom cultivate and daily practice this experience as we should. In order for us to mature as Christians and be ready for translation we must learn to *choose* it daily.

Fear sometimes holds us back from reaching inward to worship. Honesty is an integral part of worship, and it demands that we tear away the facade we have fashioned to protect ourselves and to face the depths of what we are in contrast to the greatness and majesty of God. We must be willing to shed the pride that hides our insufficiencies and accept the incredible fact that despite our unattractiveness and awkwardness God loves us and can use us in His service—not because we are so talented and clever, but because He can change and empower us by the Holy Spirit.

The Holy Spirit is the member of the Godhead most actively involved in worship. In His quiet penetrating way we can hear Him above the loudest clamor. After Jesus returned to heaven, the Holy Spirit took the place of Jesus as guide and instructor for those who follow God.

Jesus described the kind of worship that God desires from His followers during His conversation with the woman at the well in Samaria. Not the mixed worship of the Samaritans, the intellectual worship of the Jews, the place we worship, or even the form we use in prayer, but the spiritual uplifting of the creature's heart to the Creator in humility and contrition is what Jesus called "*worship in spirit and in truth.*"

How do we find the key to open the door of heaven so that we can worship God in this way?

CHAPTER 2

I Find the Key

Two sections of Scripture have been major guides in my search for an intimate relationship with God. One is the gospel story of Jesus in the New Testament; the other is the sanctuary in the Old Testament. These two halves of the same gospel weave all the rest of Scripture together, creating amazing and almost unbelievable good news!

In the Old Testament God chose Abraham and his descendants to be His special people to reflect His character to the world and to be a teaching model for the universe. When God's people found themselves slaves in Egypt, God selected Moses, a specially prepared prophet, to confront Pharaoh to free the Israelites from slavery. "Let my people go," He told the Egyptian ruler through Moses, "so that they may worship me in the desert" (Ex. 7:16). God's desire for His people is not only fellowship, intimacy between friends, but worship—the creature recognizing and adoring the Creator. Just as children respond to the love that the parent often felt before they even came into existence, so God planted in us a desire to return the love God knew before He created the first human beings.

He instructed Moses to set up the sanctuary in the wilderness so that He could dwell among them and illustrate what heaven is doing on humanity's behalf. And He filled the sanctuary with His visible glory. God knows that in order to worship Him we must first believe in Him. And in order to believe we must *see* or *hear,* either with spiritual eyes and ears or face-to-face. Patiently God led the people step by step, through Moses and other chosen leaders, to worship Him, the one true God.

The major issue has always been worship. It was so in the Garden of Eden. Whom would Adam and Eve worship—God or the serpent? The issue was worship in the wilderness—God or the golden calf? God gave the Ten Commandments to define true worship in contrast to the false worship of the surrounding nations.

Satan's final temptation in the wilderness segment of Jesus' life concerned worship. "Again, the devil took him to a very high mountain and showed him all the kingdoms of the world and their splendor. 'All this I will give you,' he said, 'if you will bow down and worship me.' Jesus said to him, 'Away from me, Satan! For it is written, "Worship the Lord your God, and serve him only"'" (Matt. 4:8-10).

The final temptation for the last generation is again worship: the Creator God or the beast?

Isn't it likely that this subject should be a major consideration of God's last-day people? Or are we confident, as the Jews were, that since we have the truth and are God's chosen people we know how to worship? Do we think that just by modernizing our public style of worship we have fulfilled the requirements of worship?

Let me continue my story. Those of you who have read my previous books know that the Lord called me as a girl and worked a wonderful change in my life. My response to His love began a joyous walk with Him, my lover and friend. However, looking back now, I can see that my love, my prayers, and my service for Him were largely sentimental. God had a long hard job ahead of Him to bring me to Christian maturity. I was sure of myself, confident that I could do anything. Patiently God walked with me as I tried and failed so many times, sometimes not even recognizing my failures, but going on to greater failures.

Finally came the greatest failure of all, the breakup of an important relationship. In heartbreak and grief I could not even find words to pray. I felt that not only had I lost an important person in my life, but also my God. My failure, my weakness, my utter inability to do *anything* for myself, overwhelmed me. Finally God could begin at the very bottom with me. He swept away my beautiful sentimental prayers and started me on the basics. And the place He began? The sanctuary services.

In desperation I searched for a firm foundation, something to hold on to, something to move forward with. No matter how often I knelt to pray, only one word escaped my lips—"Help!" Desperately I attended every prayer service I could find and listened intently to the prayers of others. I who had been a prayer leader, who had prayed eloquently and often, knew I must find a deeper meaning, a deeper faith, than I had known before.

One Sabbath afternoon I attended a prayer service led by a young Jewish man who had become a born-again Adventist Christian. He had been raised strictly as a Jew, and was steeped in the Old Testament sanctuary services. When he became a Christian he discovered that his Jewish education served as a great foundation for Christianity. In all the services of the sanctuary he found Christ and the way to salvation illustrated.

"God set up the sanctuary in the wilderness to show how He saves each human soul," he stated.

God highlighted that sentence in my mind. I was excited to consider the thought that God had *me* in mind as He outlined the plan of redemption. Growing up in the Adventist Church, I had known the sanctuary only as history, prophecy, and doctrine. For the first time I equated it with personal salvation. When the young man went on to explain that God had led him to follow the steps the priests took daily in their sanctuary work as a guide for his morning devotions, I determined to try the same kind of praying. After all, anything was better than my one-word prayer of "Help!"

My life changed. As I began in brokenness and sorrow, God lifted me up to victory and joy in the Lord. It was the same every day—recognition of my utter hopelessness and then the glorious work of God in healing and growth.

Later, while reading a familiar little book by Ellen White, I found this same personal concept put into inspired words:

"Through Christ was to be fulfilled the purpose of which the tabernacle was a symbol—that glorious building, its walls of glistening gold reflecting in rainbow hues the curtains inwrought with cherubim, the fragrance of ever-burning incense pervading all, the priests robed in spotless white, and in the deep mystery of the inner place, above the mercy seat, between the figures of the bowed, worshiping angels, the glory of the Holiest. *In all, God desired His people to read His purpose for the human soul.* It was the same purpose long afterward set forth by the apostle Paul, speaking by the Holy Spirit: 'Know ye not that ye are the temple of God, and that the Spirit of God dwelleth in you? If any man defile the temple of God, him shall God destroy; for the temple of God is holy, which temple ye are'" (*Education,* p. 36; italics supplied).

Because I talk about this experience in every one of my books, I will only briefly mention here the steps that the sanctuary reveals for personal prayer:

1. Praise to God as I enter His courts.

2. Repentance and confession at the altar of sacrifice, representing the cross.

3. Daily cleansing, rebaptism, emptying of self and sin at the laver.

4. Daily infilling of the Holy Spirit at the lampstand.

5. Growth: obedience and action at the table of shewbread.

6. Intercessory prayer for others at the altar of incense.

7. Judgment: investigation, discipline, and instruction in the Most Holy Place.

These steps changed my life, for they filtered out self-love, sentimentality, and superficiality, and focused me on moving forward in spiritual knowledge and experience.

I emphasize sanctuary prayer at the risk of sounding dogmatic and ritualistic because I truly believe that it is a gift God is presenting to His last-day people as a valuable aid in learning how to worship Him in Spirit and in truth. Of course, we do not need to word our prayers in some special way for God to hear them. There is no special sanctuary language. But most of us need some structure in order to keep our problems from looming over us, to keep us from wandering in circles, and to show us how to worship God acceptably.

Sanctuary prayer accomplishes all these things for me. It reveals to me a more complete picture of a God worthy of worship. It helps me *focus* on specifics: praise, adoration, and thankfulness to my loving God; my specific needs for forgiveness and confession; the reality of cleansing and forgiveness, Spirit infilling, and growth. Such prayer provides *order* to my thoughts. I see how God is working. Then it *moves* me along so that I don't get bogged down in self-pity or become obsessive in the self-examination necessary to recognition of truth. I can journey through the entire picture God has in mind for me each day. When I have completed my prayer I sense the reality of what God has done for me through the death of Jesus, and what He is doing for me daily through His high-priestly ministry in the heavenly sanctuary. I know that His work for me is *complete,* lacking absolutely nothing. Joy and peace accompany me as I walk hand in hand with Him throughout my day, confident that I will hear His voice. What a climate for worship!

I know that I am not alone in feeling the need for some sort of structure for my prayers, because I have read of many useful aids to prayer. Many center on the acronym ACTS: adoration, confession, thanksgiving, and supplication. Journaling in prayer is a popular way today to structure prayer. Following the steps of the Lord's Prayer in Matthew 6 is another. In fact, the prayer Jesus taught His disciples follows closely the same outline God illustrated for the Hebrews in the sanctuary services. I use the sanctuary illustration rather than the prayer in Matthew 6 as my guide because of the openness of the entire sanctuary sequence that leads me to greater understanding of God's daily work in my salvation.

I believe the prayer models I have mentioned above—and others—are a great blessing to many people. At the same time I also recognize that *any* structure runs the danger of becoming a form rather than true prayer. Thus I empathize with a young woman who told me that she had tried sanctuary prayer, but after a time it had become—to use her own words—"nauseating" to her. When our prayers become rote they become nauseating to God also! (See Rev. 3:15, 16.) But I believe that just as God admonished the church in Ephesus to revive their first love, we also need to revive our prayers so that the warmth of faith and love will accompany them. Our prayers need to become hot with the presence of the Holy Spirit.

Sanctuary prayer actually protects me from the deadliness of ritual that we often find in prayer because it never closes me in, but is always open. It can vary widely yet still follow the form. When I arrived in Norway I was delighted to find that the pastor who had invited me followed the steps of sanctuary prayer for his own personal devotions. A large man, six foot four or five, physical exercise is crucial to his well-being. Telling us that he prays as he runs a seven-mile route every morning, he explained that he has special places where he stops to pray for each step of sanctuary prayer, beginning with a large open place in which he enters the courtyard with praise. Wherever I go to speak, I am thrilled to hear of the many varieties of sanctuary prayer.

One of the dangers inherent in using any illustration is that we may focus upon the illustration rather than on the reality it is seeking to reflect. We need to focus continually on the sanctuary in heaven in which Jesus is doing the high-priestly work for us. Although our earth is clearly the center of heaven's focus, our attention must always center on heaven. Sanctuary prayer is not just a structure for prayer, but a teaching aid. It should not just lead us into the study of the Old Testament sanctuary that Moses built in the days of the Israelites, but should direct us to a greater understanding of God and into a deeper, more spiritual worship experience. Sanctuary prayer is not designed to be limited to specific segments of time, but should change our entire thinking habits.

As I began praying through the steps of the sanctuary by entering His gates with praise I really had no idea of how to praise God properly. I would simply thank the Lord for His personal blessings to me. Early on I began to be uncomfortable with this self-centered praise. As a result, I studied the Psalms for examples of praise, knowing that the priests chanted and sang many of these very verses as they began their services each morning. I started to see that although they often mention personal praise—God's intervention in human lives—yet glory to God the Creator is always the focal point of praise. So I began choosing verses of praise to the Creator that centered on His omnipotence, and used them for my personal praise prayers. One of my first attempts at this was through Exodus 15:11:

> "Who among the gods is like you, O Lord?
> Who is like you—
> majestic in holiness,
> awesome in glory,
> working wonders?"

This verse lifted my heart up toward God, away from myself, and gave me a glimpse of an awesome, majestic, creative God, not just a God responding to my need. He became a God who stood apart from me and yet somehow wanted to be a part of me.

> "For this is what the high and lofty One says—
> he who lives forever, whose name is holy:
> 'I live in a high and holy place,
> but also with him who is contrite
> and lowly in spirit,
> to revive the spirit of the lowly
> and to revive the heart of the contrite'" (Isa. 57:15).

Throughout Scripture we find its writers continually praising God for preserving the Israelites through their numerous adventures. But always their praise lifts God up to the highest place. God's deep desire for me was that I go on from self-centered praise to true worship that centers upon God.

My struggle with praise to God for Himself alone originated in the fact that I am basically self-centered. It is impossible for me to eliminate self even when praising God. But as I reach out toward God, longing for the deepest relationship with Him that is possible for a human being to experience, God has increased my understanding. Although it is true that we must stretch beyond ourselves to praise a God big enough to inhabit the entire universe, yet He is pleased to have our praise come through the vessels of our humanity and in our individual way. Ellen White puts it this way:

"Every individual has a life distinct from all others, and an experience differing essentially from theirs. God desires that our praise shall ascend to Him, marked by our own individuality. These precious acknowledgments to the praise of the glory of His grace, when supported by a Christlike life, have an irresistible power that works for the salvation of souls" (*The Desire of Ages,* p. 347).

One day as I was reading the chapter "Transformed by Grace" in *The Acts of the Apostles* I felt an intense desire to be transformed by the same power that changed the apostles of Jesus. I read of John, naturally resentful and ambitious, whom the Holy Spirit made so much like the Master he loved that God could trust him to write the important book of Revelation, which opens to the world the glorious culmination of redemption. "He yielded his resentful, ambitious temper to the molding power of Christ," Ellen White wrote of John, "and divine love wrought in him a transformation of character" (p. 557).

As I read and reread that sentence about the apostle John, yearning for the same experience in my life, the Holy Spirit rewrote that sentence just for me. As clearly as with my visual eyes I saw the words, "She (Carrol) yielded her self-indulgent disposition to the molding power of Christ, and divine love wrought in her a transformation of character."

I've never forgotten that moment and that promise, and I know by faith that God is daily doing that work in me. With the power of the Holy Spirit I am enabled to worship God in a way that pleases Him.

God is dependent upon our intelligent cooperation with Him in every step of His work of salvation for us. Since He uses no force other than love, He can proceed only as we cooperate with Him. And so sometimes our progress is slow. But God is willing to take the time and patiently cover the same ground again and again until we understand. Here is where the sanctuary illustration has been such a blessing to me. It has clarified for me the exact path I need to take and has shown me the futility of my pride and self-sufficiency. It has highlighted the important issues and settled the less important into their places.

As morning by morning I walk through the steps of praise, repentance and confession, and cleansing and healing, I arrive at the lampstand eager to be Spirit-filled, to receive God's gifts. It was at the lampstand that I became aware of the true key to worship.

I was almost afraid as I came to the lampstand the first few times I tried sanctuary prayer. Sanctuary prayer had lifted me out of my pit of darkness, and exciting things had begun happening in my life. Daily I experienced God's power. Although I believed that God desired to give the Holy Spirit in fullness to His followers, yet I wished I knew just what that would mean in my life. I was delighted with the joy of a living relationship with God, but was I ready for anything really spectacular? The Holy Spirit was a powerful entity. Would I speak in tongues, as did the apostles at Pentecost? Would I be lifted from place to place as had happened to Philip and others in Bible times? Would I fall to the floor, "slain by the Spirit," as were many of the early Methodists and some of our own Adventist pioneers?

As much as I wanted the full presence of God in my life, I was fearful of just what that meant.

As you can see, the practice of sanctuary prayer introduced me to subjects I had scarcely noted before! But when God raises a question in our minds He always has an answer. As I investigated scriptures about the Spirit I discovered that God has not left us ignorant of what the Holy Spirit desires to do in our lives. Isaiah 11:1-5 is a prophecy of the marvelous way God the Father and God the Holy Spirit would provide for God the Son when He became a weak human being. The Holy Spirit not only played a vital role in the birth of Christ as a man, but He was also wholly responsible for the daily life of victory that the human Jesus lived. When I realized this I sensed an immediate peace. Surely I can trust the Holy Spirit to work in my own life the same way.

> "A shoot will come up from the stump of Jesse;
>   from his roots a Branch will bear fruit.
> The Spirit of the Lord will rest on him—
>   the Spirit of wisdom and of understanding,
>   the Spirit of counsel and of power,
>   the Spirit of knowledge and of the fear of the Lord—
> and he will delight in the fear of the Lord.
> He will not judge by what he sees with his eyes,
>   or decide by what he hears with his ears;
> but with righteousness he will judge the needy,
>   with justice he will give decisions
>   for the poor of the earth.
> He will strike the earth with the rod of his mouth;
>   with the breath of his lips he will slay the wicked.
> Righteousness will be his belt
>   and faithfulness the sash around his waist" (Isa.
>   11:1-5).

If Jesus, the Son of God, as a human did not trust His own

ears or eyes but depended upon the guidance of the Holy Spirit, that is what I want to do too. God desires to give us the necessary knowledge, wisdom, and understanding to walk with God just as He did Jesus. He wants to endow us with power for victory and the ability to hear His constant counsel. The Lord will fill us with the same "fear of the Lord" that so delighted Jesus as a man—awe, adoration, love, and submission for God. It will cause us to "delight" in obedience and worship just as did Jesus. Whatever we know will please God we will immediately want to do. Just as Jesus said of His Father, "I delight to do Your will" and "I always do what pleases My Father," so we will also reach out in loving obedience to our Father, worshiping at His feet in adoration and submission.

> "The Lord is exalted, for he dwells on high;
> he will fill Zion with justice and righteousness.
> He will be the sure foundation for your times,
> a rich store of salvation and wisdom and knowledge;
> *the fear of the Lord* is the key to this treasure"
> (Isa. 33:5, 6).

It was a delight to discover the key to worship clearly identified as I studied about the sanctuary! No wonder David said, "I have seen you in the sanctuary" (Ps. 63:2).

Since God says that the "fear of the Lord" is the key to what the Spirit has to offer, I began searching for Bible verses about this wonderful attribute of worship. In studying them, I discovered that by far the majority of the verses, rather than defining "fear of the Lord," instead refer to its results.

"The fear of the Lord is the beginning of knowledge" (Prov. 1:7).

"The fear of the Lord teaches a man wisdom" (Prov. 15:33).

"The fear of the Lord is the beginning of wisdom" (Prov. 9:10).

"To fear the Lord is to hate evil" (Prov. 8:13).

"Through the fear of the Lord a man avoids evil" (Prov. 16:6).

"The fear of the Lord leads to life: then one rests content, untouched by trouble" (Prov. 19:23).

"Humility and the fear of the Lord bring wealth and honor and life" (Prov. 22:4).

The awe, respect, and submission due God the Father was the delight of His Son. How much more should it be our great privilege to bow before our Lord in worship!

So much of Christian living seems subjective. It's hard to judge one's own motives. And it is so easy for worship to become ritual or form while our hearts are preoccupied with self—and we may not even recognize it. Thus it is good to find a key—something that seems tangible, something that opens the door, something that shows us the way to worship. Following the steps of the sanctuary layout has proven to be my key to personal worship.

As I share these concepts with you I am not claiming to have all the answers. Along with the young woman who told me that she found the routine of sanctuary prayer "nauseating," I also sometimes struggle with restlessness, self-indulgence, and the deadliness of ritual and rote. But God is showing me more and more ways to resist distraction and center in on worship. More and more I respond to God's call to worship, emptying my mind of self-centeredness, not asking Him for anything, but bowing at His feet in total submission, recognizing my unworthiness and His holiness.

When I say "not asking for anything," I am not saying that when we learn to worship we will never request anything from God ever again. After all, God delights to give. We are instructed to ask. In fact, He wants us to ask for far more than we do. What I mean is that in our relationship with God we are content to simply rest in His goodness. We would not be upset if He never gave us anything ever again. Instead, we hunger and thirst only after *Him*. Perhaps David is the greatest example in worship as he pours forth his psalms of yearning:

"As the deer pants for streams of water,
    so my soul pants for you, O God.
My soul thirsts for God, for the living God.
    When can I go and meet with God?" (Ps. 42:1, 2).

"O God, you are my God,
    earnestly I seek you;
my soul thirsts for you,
    my body longs for you,
    in a dry and weary land
where there is no water" (Ps. 63:1).

"My heart says of you, 'Seek his face!'
    Your face, Lord, I will seek" (Ps. 27:8).

Worship is the creature's heart response to God's purity and love. All we long for is the face of Jesus. It is almost as though God and I dwell alone in the midst of awesome silence in which only the bright light of God's countenance shines. It satisfies every need, comforts every grief, fulfills every hope.

After a period of worship, of reaching out to God in praise and adoration, I am strengthened to intercede for others, to minister. As I feel the touch of the live coal from heaven's altar upon my lips, I cry with the young Isaiah, "Here am I, send me!" (Isa. 6:8).

But worship does not restrict itself to quiet devotional times. Worship must become our lifestyle.

Summary

I believe two sections of Scripture guide us to understand God's great desire to have an intimate relationship with humanity: the gospel accounts of Jesus in the New Testament, and the sanctuary in the Old Testament. Both show us the way to worship God in spirit and in truth.

When God chose Abraham and his descendants to be His

special people, He met the need they had to worship. He rescued them from slavery in Egypt so that they could find freedom to worship Him. "Let my people go," He told Pharaoh, "so that they may worship me in the desert" (Ex. 7:16).

Worship has always been the major issue in choosing whom we will serve. In Eden: the God who had created humanity, or the serpent? In the wilderness: the God who had parted the Red Sea, or the golden calf? The Lord gave the Ten Commandments to define true worship in contrast to the false worship of other peoples. The final temptation for the last generation will be worship: the Creator God, or the beast?

Isn't it likely that worship should be a major consideration of God's last-day people?

One key to how to worship in spirit and in truth appears in the sanctuary illustration God instructed Moses to set up in the wilderness. Portraying to us how God saves each human soul, it shows us in detail the intimate work He desires to do for each of us to lead us to worship Him. Through the Holy Spirit we are able to bow low before God in the fear of the Lord—reverent submission to God in all things. Following the steps of the sanctuary service in personal prayer will lead us to worship Him in spirit (from the very depths of our hearts) and in truth (intelligent and biblically based understanding of what God is doing to save His people).

Worship is the creature's heart response to the purity and love of God and leads us to service for Him and others.

CHAPTER 3

Lifestyle Worship

Nothing brings me greater joy than recognizing the voice of the Holy Spirit in my mind. Even His corrections are something to anticipate. I feel like the prophet Jeremiah as He exclaimed, "When your words came, I ate them; they were my joy and my heart's delight, for I bear your name, O Lord God Almighty" (Jer. 15:16).

Like Jeremiah, whenever God reveals to me specific areas in which my thinking differs from His or in which my lifestyle borders on disobedience, I turn to Him in repentance, asking for forgiveness. I realize that unless the way I live represents God, I cannot bring glory to Him. In the past I would finish my prayer with almost a sense of elation, positive that once I had seen the problem, repented, and confessed my sin, surely that blemish had vanished from my life.

Only recently has it dawned on me that all the things the Lord has spoken to me about—things which I repented of and confessed as sin—are *still* problems in my life. Although they may immediately disappear and not reappear for months or even years, given the right climate—sickness, discouragement, sorrow, idleness, or stress—they turn up to haunt me.

"There's something wrong here, Lord!" I exclaimed in deep concern one morning during my prayer time. "You showed me the error of my ways, and I sincerely repented and confessed these sins. Trusting You to bury them in the bottom of the sea,

I thought my weaknesses were supposed to become my strengths. But it's obvious that I am still weak in all these areas. Oh, Lord, I long to repent so deeply that I never need repent of these same sins again!"

Patiently God instructed me. "When I call these things to your mind, it is only the *beginning*," He told me, "not the end. My purpose is to impress upon you that it is high time that *we*—you and I—begin seriously working on these areas."

"You mean they can't be forgotten?" I questioned. "I have to keep them in my mind all the time?" I was aghast at my responsibility—and terribly burdened.

God explained that He would carry that burden. "I'll keep them in My mind. Your job is to abide in Me, listen for My voice, and *choose* to cooperate with Me."

"But sometimes I seem so hard of hearing," I protested hopelessly, "and I override my conscience without even really thinking. It is only later that I realize what I have done."

Years of habitual sinning take a toll. They burn paths into the mind and the body. Oh, how I longed for God to take away all remembrance of past indulgences and start me out with a fresh, unmarred mind. I knew God could do it too. He heals alcoholics and drug addicts, often miraculously removing all desire for the substance. Surely He could do the same for my self-indulgence. Why wasn't He doing it?

As I ended my prayertime that morning with no final answer to my questions I picked up the Sabbath school lesson quarterly to review the current lesson with my mind still mulling my need for total healing. We had just begun the study of the book of Judges, and the second lesson covered Judges 2:6 to Judges 3:6.

When I began reading I was amazed to find God speaking to me in the book of Judges! Here were the Israelites, God's chosen people, finally in the Promised Land. Moses, of course, had died just before they entered the land, but Joshua had led them in battle, driving out the enemy and taking possession of the Promised Land. Now Joshua too was dead. The people, a generation born in the land, had never been slaves. They had never participated in the battles for Canaan and were weak and self-indulgent. But enemies still occupied the land. What to do? Would God drive their enemies out by Himself, as He so easily could—and had already promised to do contingent upon their faithful worship of Him and their abstinence from idolatry?

"No," God announces, "I will not drive these enemies out. I am leaving them to *test* My people."

God's people had not proved faithful. They sometimes joined the pagans in idol worship. He had some lessons for His people to learn. Judges 3:2 says, "He did this only to teach *warfare* to the descendants of the Israelites who had not had previous battle experience."

Suddenly I realized why God did not just miraculously take away all my self-indulgent tendencies. Like the Israelites in Judges who did not share in the battles for the Promised Land, I needed battle experience. The only way to receive experience is through living it. God was giving me the opportunity in peaceful times to learn warfare by personal participation in overcoming my ingrained sins. The experience will be important to me as I face the troubled days ahead.

Of course, no way can I fight these battles by myself. The battle is between Christ and Satan. I'm not even a major contestant. But I am a key one. Without my choice to obey God in every intimate part of my life, the battle cannot be won. The strength is not mine, but God's. My part is to give Him my will and fasten my faith wholly in Him. God's forgiveness is totally unlike the magic I so delighted in reading about during my younger years. Zap, sin and all my sinful tendencies are gone. But God has great plans for the human race—He desires for us to develop characters that will endure for eternity. The image of God—which He originally created in Adam and Eve—He plans to redevelop so thoroughly in each of us that we resemble Him in thought and action.

Satan is unable to create anything. His magic only counterfeits God's power. God never uses magic, He deals only in miracles. Magic is a deception, while miracles are the reality. The miracle of forgiveness is mine immediately upon my confession of sin. Then comes the miracle of daily overcoming, something God can accomplish only with my constant cooperation.

And that involves warfare!

In the past I have read statements intimating that the time should come in the life of a Christian when our wills are so identified with Christ's will that our desires will be identical with God's desires. The choices we make will be just what God wants us to do. In my love of magic I thought such an experience should happen immediately upon my acceptance of His rebuke. Now God was showing me that this occurs only after my faithful practice makes warfare habitual. My desires will become so thoroughly united with God's desires that they will be identical. But this will be true only as I daily put into practice the warfare tactics He is teaching me. He promises that all the things He has brought to my attention are things He will give me victory on *as I cooperate with Him moment by moment.* The work He has begun in me He will finish as I abide in Him. My responsibility is the abiding—which includes deliberate moment-by-moment choices—but even that I cannot do alone. He holds me, comforts me, strengthens me, with a hand that will never let go.

Lest you wonder if I have forgotten that this is a book about worship, let me correlate what I am talking about with the subject of worship. Only one way exists to worship God truly, and that is with our *whole* hearts. Yet most of us have divided hearts, something Scripture strongly reprimands. The writer of the Epistle of James portrays our divided hearts as "double-minded" and says that such a person is "unstable" in all that they do (James 1:6-8). David prays:

"Teach me your way, O Lord,

> and I will walk in your truth;
>   give me an *undivided heart,*
>   that I may fear [worship] your name.
> I will praise you, O Lord my God,
>   with all my heart;
> I will glorify your name forever" (Ps. 86:11, 12).

We *cannot* acceptably worship God in purity and holiness until we do so with our *whole* hearts. God's business is to purge us of double-mindedness, digging down into the very depths of our minds so that we willingly and intelligently choose Him in every area of our lives. But God cannot do this without our complete consent and cooperation. We must personally battle our inherited and cultivated tendencies to evil.

It has taken a long time for me to realize that God's voice in His judgment work in the most holy place in heaven, as He points out areas in which I am weak, is the *beginning,* not the *end,* of the battle. My response should not only be repentance and confession, but I should continually resist my deep sins— my individual tendencies to dishonor God.

Years ago when I began memorizing whole chapters of Scripture I frequently chose the Psalms. But I began to be concerned with what I termed "the bloodthirsty psalms," in which David shouts vindictive threats against his enemies. Psalms that spoke especially to my heart would be "spoiled" (as I saw it!) with David's thirst for the death of his enemies. I was memorizing Psalm 139, but stopped in alarm when I came to verse 19: "If only you would slay the wicked, O God!"

David's attitude, as I remembered Christ's counsel to love our enemies, made me extremely uncomfortable.

This really isn't the Christian response, David! I thought. The only way I could finish memorizing the psalm was to leave out the four verses I deemed unsuitable. But as I went on to more psalms I found verses even more deadly. How could I reconcile such sentiments with a loving God? I remember mentioning my concern to Glenn Coon (author of *The ABC's of Bible Prayer*), who had always been an encouragement to me in my prayer life. Coon admitted that he too had wondered about those verses.

"But then I read over the stories of David's life and how he treated his personal enemies. He spared King Saul's life when he could have killed him in the cave. It seems that the enemies he wished to be dead were the enemies of God, not his own," Coon explained.

I reexamined Psalm 139. Yes, David said, "Do I not hate those who hate you, O Lord . . . ?" (verse 21).

What about me? Who were the enemies in my life? At that time I could find no human beings who were my personal enemies. My most distracting enemies were certain sins that I truly wished God would slay! Surely these sins were God's enemies, too, for they continually brought dishonor to Him through me. I decided to approach the Psalms with my sins in mind rather than people as enemies. This way I could even appreciate the bloodthirsty psalms. I could match David's vehemence as I called down fire from heaven upon my besetting sins!

Now God was asking me to get bloodthirsty! It was time I learned warfare. I began to search the Bible for battle tactics and discovered that God uses warfare terminology throughout Scripture. So much for peace! There is a time for peace and a time for war. Now is the time for war. Who is my enemy? My battle is with the flesh (my ingrained sins), the world (which seeks to force us into its pattern), and the devil (who prowls around like a roaring lion).

"For though we live in the world, we do not wage war as the world does. The weapons we fight with are not the weapons of the world. On the contrary, they have divine power to demolish strongholds. We demolish argument and every pretension that sets itself up against the knowledge of God, and we take captive every thought to make it obedient to Christ" (2 Cor. 10:3-5).

I need to learn how to battle as a Christian, how to "demolish strongholds" and "arguments," and how to "take captive every thought." In my Bible search I discovered five major warfare tactics: *submit to God, resist the devil, flee from idolatry, obey God and worship Him,* and *watch and pray.* As Christians we need not only to have Bible promises ready as weapons, but also to recognize the principles involved.

The first warfare tactic is *submit to God.* It is the only way to prepare to fight spiritual war, for without God we have no power.

"Submit yourselves, then, to God. Resist the devil, and he will flee from you. Come near to God and he will come near to you. Wash your hands, you sinners, and purify your hearts, you double-minded. Grieve, mourn and wail. Change your laughter to mourning and your joy to gloom. Humble yourselves before the Lord, and he will lift you up" (James 4:7-10).

It was a difficult verse for me to comprehend. Surely God didn't want me to deliberately go around grieving, mourning, and wailing! So I put it into the culture James wrote from. The Jews were a highly expressive people who wailed and mourned loudly to show their grief. What James tells me in these verses is that I'd better be serious about this battle. No one will find a relationship with God unless he or she is wholehearted in his or her desire for God. In no way can I ever resist the devil until I have submitted my life completely to Him.

When the temptation comes, it is too late to submit to God. The only way for victory is *already* to be wholly yielded. Every morning as I enter the courtyard of heaven by faith, I humble myself before the cross of Christ, giving my entire life to Him, telling Him how much I desire Him. I confess my sinfulness at the altar of sacrifice, asking God to impress upon me the seriousness of my sins (that's the grieving, mourning, wailing, and gloom that James talks about!). But then I rejoice that God willingly forgives my sins (that's when God lifts me up!). Only then can I resist the devil.

Part of my submission to God is to wear willingly the special armor He has provided for all Christians as a protection against temptation. When young David went out to fight the giant Goliath, King Saul offered him his royal armor. But when the shepherd lad tried it on, it was obviously much too large and would be a hindrance rather than a help. So David went to meet Goliath clothed only in his simple shepherd's garment. Visibly, that is. We know that he was wearing the same armor God asks all of us to wear. You see, when God gives those who trust in Him His armor, He fits it perfectly for each one. He asks us to wear it at all times, not even taking it off for sleep. His armor is not only protective, but fashioned for aggressive warfare.

Growing up, I had the distinct feeling that the church was a club for the righteous. It was refreshing to me as an adult when I began to hear that it was a hospital for both saints and sinners. But now I find an even greater truth. Neil Anderson writes that the church is more than just a hospital for the healing of the saints:

"The church is not a hospital; *it's a military outpost under orders to storm the gates of hell*. Every believer is on active duty, called to take part in fulfilling the Great Commission (Matt. 28:19, 20). Thankfully the church has an infirmary where we can minister to the weak and wounded, and that ministry is necessary. But our real purpose is to be change agents in the world, taking a stand, living by faith and accomplishing something for God" (Neil Anderson with Joanne Anderson, *Daily in Christ* [Harvest House Publishers]; italics supplied).

We should consciously wear the armor Paul spoke of in Ephesians 6:14-17:

1. "The belt of truth." Truth and error grow closely together. In fact, Ellen White tells us that error grows upon the tree of truth because it cannot stand alone (*Evangelism,* p. 589). This is an important principle to remember as we read or listen to sermons. I must carefully examine what others present to me as truth and weed out error so that I can be protected by the belt of truth.

2. "The breastplate of righteousness." Our trust must not

be in our own righteousness, something God views as "filthy rags." The Hebrew phrase from Isaiah 64:6 actually refers to blood-soaked menstrual cloths, an abhorrent thought in any culture. In contrast, we discover that the blood of Christ is the basis of our redemption and the pure robe of His righteousness is our protection.

3. The shoes of the "readiness that comes from the gospel of peace." These shoes are the same sandals Jesus wore as He traveled all over Judea, healing and teaching (Isa. 52:7), and that led Him eventually to the cross. Such shoes give us "firm-footed stability, the promptness and the readiness" we need to stand up for the Lord (Eph. 6:15, Amplified). I like these shoes. They are the shoes I wear wherever I go to speak. But I also need to remember to wear them at home, when I shop, when I work, and even on vacation.

4. "The shield of faith." I can remember being concerned about this part of the armor as I realized that my faith often developed holes that would surely allow the darts of the enemy to pass through. I prayed for greater and stronger faith. But one morning as I was walking and memorizing Psalm 91, I discovered something vital. "His faithfulness will be your shield," I recited. *His* faith, not mine, is my shield! I was so excited about this that I nearly fell off the curb! Every part of the armor God asks me to wear is His. Jesus guarantees the protection. It has no weak spots, no holes. The shield of faith is the same strong faith that Jesus demonstrated throughout His earthly life and by which He was victorious on the cross. Such faith is the gold tried in the fire that Jesus counsels His last church to buy (Rev. 3:18; 1 Peter 1:7). Jack Sequiera calls it "saving faith." Saving faith has three important elements: "(1) *knowing* the truth as it is in Jesus; (2) *believing* the truth as it is in Jesus; and (3) *obeying* the truth as it is in Jesus" (Jack Sequiera, *Beyond Belief,* pp. 91, 92).

5. "The helmet of salvation." I like to add "assurance of salvation" to this helmet. So many of us vacillate between being confident of our salvation and feeling that in no way are we

going to make it! If salvation is to make a real difference in my personal life, I need the assurance that I possess it. I remember reading once in a little booklet, "When I look at myself I don't see how in the world I can ever be saved, but when I look at Jesus I don't see how in the world I can ever be lost."

Jesus promised: "My sheep listen to my voice; I know them, and they follow me. I give them eternal life, and they shall never perish; no one can snatch them out of my hand. My Father, who has given them to me, is greater than all; no one can snatch them out of my Father's hand. I and the Father are one" (John 10:27-30).

The key to assurance for our personal salvation is understanding that Jesus worked out salvation for all humanity by His life and death here on earth, and that He offers it to us as a free gift. Testing ourselves by what we do or feel to see if we are saved is not a valid test. Our "doings" and our emotions will always fall short of God's perfection. However, we can check our progress in sanctification by examining our actions, for they reveal if we are walking in the Spirit. Christ gives the garment of His perfect righteousness to us as a gift when we are born again, and it remains ours until we reject it by rebellion and willful disobedience.

Our works are always for the purpose of giving glory to the Father.

Assurance of salvation is a helmet that not only protects us from the enemy on the outside, but most of all, from the enemy of self-accusation. When Satan tells me that I am a hypocrite, that I am not really saved, that I have no hope of changing, and that I am unworthy to be a worker for Christ, the helmet of salvation provides assurance of my salvation. Wearing it brings me peaceful sleep and joyful waking.

6. "The sword of the Spirit which is the word of God." "For the word of God is living and active. Sharper than any double-edged sword, it penetrates even to dividing soul and spirit, joints and marrow; it judges the thoughts and attitudes of the

heart. Nothing in all creation is hidden from God's sight. Everything is uncovered and laid bare before the eyes of him to whom we must give account.

"Therefore, since we have a great high priest who has gone through the heavens, Jesus the Son of God, let us hold firmly to the faith we profess. For we do not have a high priest who is unable to sympathize with our weaknesses, but we have one who has been tempted in every way, just as we are—yet was without sin. Let us then approach the throne of grace with confidence, so that we may receive mercy and find grace to help us in our time of need" (Heb. 4:12-16).

Although we put on this armor initially for protection and often view it as primarily defensive, yet as we come to pick up the sword we see that God has fashioned the armor to enable us to attack the enemy. With the Sword of the Spirit, the Word of God, we can examine ourselves to see if we are in right standing with God, identify the path of obedience, and wield the sword to storm the gates of hell.

7. Intercessory prayer for the saints. Because Paul ends his simile of armor with the sword, we often forget that he really lists a perfect seven for warfare. Prayer for each other is one of our greatest weapons against the devil. Like the sword, intercession is offensive warfare, rather than defensive.

It is almost as though when we put on the armor we finally become strong enough to fight offensively. *The weakest saint upon their knees in prayer makes Satan tremble.*

Paul tells us that if we submit to wearing this armor, we will stand, no matter what evil assails us. Nothing can cause us to fall (Eph. 6:10-18). Yes, all of the above are under the heading of submission! In another place Jesus describes submission as wearing His yoke (Matt. 11:28-30). Submission to God is always a first step toward victory, a first tactic for warfare.

The second warfare tactic is to *resist the devil*. "Be self-controlled and alert. Your enemy the devil prowls around like a roaring lion looking for someone to devour. Resist him, standing firm in the faith" (1 Peter 5:8, 9).

I have found several biblical ways to resist the devil:

Quote Scripture. As a Man Jesus set us an example when He confronted the devil in the wilderness with memorized words from the Bible.

Prayer. Again Jesus is our best example as He prayed in Gethsemene for strength to resist His own will, but to accept the Father's will. When Christians begin to realize that their intimacy with God guarantees moment by moment connection with Him, they will see that their every thought can be a prayer. The apostle Paul tells us to pray without ceasing. When faced with special temptation, our prayers should be specific and fervent.

Praise God aloud, either in song or spoken word. God instructed the leaders of the Israelites to send musicians to play instruments and a choir to sing praises before the armies of Israel as they went forth into battle. When Paul and Silas spent a night in prison they sang praises to God. The result was the conversion of the jailer and his family (Acts 16:22-34).

Make a verbal confession of faith in Jesus. We should declare it aloud, as Satan cannot read our minds. Perhaps you could say, "I believe that Jesus Christ, Son of the living God, came to earth, was born of a virgin, lived a sinless life, died on the cross of Calvary for my sins, rose the third day, ascended up into heaven, where He now sits on the throne of the Majesty on high, ever living to make intercession for me as my High Priest and Saviour. One day soon He is coming to earth again to take me home to live with Him throughout eternity."

The sermons of the apostles often included a confession of their faith that Jesus was the Son of God as they spoke before an unbelieving throng. Satan and his angels will not stay where God's people glorify Jesus.

The third warfare tactic is to *flee from idolatry.* "Therefore, my dear friends, flee from idolatry" (1 Cor. 10:14). "The name of the Lord is a strong tower; the righteous run to it and are safe" (Prov. 18:10).

Idolatry is putting anything before God in our affections. It can be work or pleasure. Because God created us and redeemed us, He must always have first place in our hearts. We should determine to run from anything that tempts us to put it in first place. A good biblical example is Joseph, who fled from Potiphar's wife rather than risk falling under her seduction (Gen. 39:12). When we know we are weak in certain areas, we need, as far as possible, to avoid temptation in those areas. The other day I was in a store walking down an aisle containing items that constantly tempt me. In my ear I heard a whisper, "Flee!" My first reaction was to laugh at myself—*flee* is definitely not a word I normally use. But since the word had a scriptural basis, I decided that very likely it was the Holy Spirit speaking to me. I hurried past those displays and thanked God for His warning. We need to train ourselves to look for ways to escape such temptations.

"No temptation has seized you except what is common to man. And God is faithful; he will not let you be tempted beyond what you can bear. But when you are tempted, He will also provide a way out so that you can stand up under it" (1 Cor. 10:13).

(Often my problem with looking for some avenue of escape is that I don't really want to find it! Yet if I am open to the Spirit's voice, He will reveal even this to me. My only safety from the tricky double-mindedness of my own heart is to daily ask God to renew my mind in His likeness so that I will always desire to do what pleases Him the most, serving Him with my whole heart.)

The fourth warfare tactic is to *obey God and keep His commandments.* God gave the ten commandment law for our protection—His law acts as a hedge around us. Obedience to God guards us against sin. When Christians walk in obedience, the blood of Jesus surrounds them and protects them from dark powers. But unconfessed sin in the life of the Christian makes a gap in the circle, allowing evil to enter (Corrie ten Boom, *Tramp for the Lord,* p. 170). We can find numerous examples, both negative and positive, in Scripture.

Negative: Ananias and Sapphira harbored the sin of covetousness and fell under greater temptation. Balaam, once a true prophet, also succumbed to the sin of covetousness and became a byword in history for unfaithfulness. King Saul, though God had made him a new creature, cherished jealousy and pride, and the door opened for murder and rebellion. King David allowed lust to enter his life, and he committed murder. Fortunately, he repented, asked for forgiveness, and went on to a righteous life.

Positive: Daniel and his three friends were careful even in the little things, such as eating and drinking, and God protected them against pride and disobedience in the big things. Joseph fled from temptation, and God sheltered him from pride and retaliation.

The fifth warfare tactic is to *watch and pray*. Jesus said to Peter, James, and John in Gethsemane, "Watch and pray so that you will not fall into temptation. The spirit is willing, but the body is weak" (Matt. 26:41).

Ellen White tells us that had the disciples stayed awake and joined Jesus in prayer that night they would have had the faith to accompany Jesus to the cross and would have been spared deep heartache and disappointment. They would have had the faith to believe that He would rise again on the third day as He had prophesied. Learning to watch and pray with Jesus will help us to avoid temptation.

"Pray much. While at your work let your heart be uplifted to God. When you have committed to God the keeping of your soul, do not go away and act contrary to the prayer you have made. Watch as well as pray, lest you be overcome with temptation. Resist the first inclination to do wrong. Pray in your heart, 'Jesus, help me; preserve me from evil,' and then do what you know Christ would be pleased to have you do" (*That I May Know Him,* p. 41).

Part of watching is guarding. "Above all else, guard your

heart, for it is the wellspring of life" (Prov. 4:23).

The heart the wise man was talking about is really our minds and the thoughts we cherish in them. Jesus talked about these same things. "The good man brings good things out of the good stored up in his heart, and the evil man brings evil things out of the evil stored up in his heart. For out of the overflow of his heart his mouth speaks" (Luke 6:45).

Experience has taught me that I need to carefully guard my mind from storing up grievances and resentments because such thoughts will eventually overflow in my words and actions (not even to mention what they do to my peace of mind!). The author of Hebrews tells us that we should "make every effort to live in peace with all men and to be holy; without holiness no one will see the Lord. See to it that no one misses the grace of God and that no bitter root grows up to cause trouble and defile many" (Heb. 12:14, 15).

An important part of watching is keeping the hurts of life from rooting themselves in our hearts to flower in bitterness, resentment, or self-pity. The only way I know to uproot such harmful thoughts from my mind is to consciously and deliberately give them over to God in prayer, accepting by faith that even the most hurtful experiences in life God will work out for my good and to His glory. It calls for an aggressive act of giving up rather than a passive act of acceptance. I say this because it is possible that if we passively accept a hurt, it may dig in deeper rather than get uprooted.

As we learn God's warfare tactics we will find a change in our lifestyle, a new depth to our worship. God must have a people, a group, a church, to whom He can bring all His people on earth together to light up the whole earth with His glory in preparation for His second coming. Such a group will not only understand and live out Bible truth—righteousness by faith alone, what happens to the dead, worship on the seventh day, end-time prophecies, and the second coming of Christ—their very lifestyle will be worship. They will obey God's commandments from the heart and will resemble Him in the way they treat each other, welcoming seeking sinners into their midst. God's people may not all worship publicly in the same way or sing the same hymns of praise; they will not all use the same formulas for prayer or speak the same language. But they will glorify God because of their whole-hearted adoration of the Creator of the universe. It will be revealed by their love.

Worship doesn't just belong in church or in our private devotions. It must become a part of our daily life. True worship will bring about a decided change in our lifestyle. (Read God's counsel to the Jewish people in Isaiah 58.) The people who will receive the power of the latter rain will be those who have loving hearts as well as a deep commitment to the body of Christ.

John Garmo describes what he calls "lifestyle worship" as having three components. He illustrates this with two overlapping horizontal rectangles. The first rectangle he calls "loving," the second "serving." The overlapping portion forms a smaller rectangle that he terms "abiding." The first rectangle, loving, involves mainly the attitudes of our hearts. The second rectangle, serving, appears in our actions. The overlapping abiding is in both our attitudes and in our actions (*Lifestyle Worship* [Thomas Nelson, 1993], p. 25).

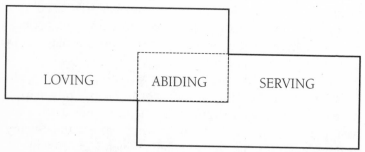

Perhaps this threesome—loving, serving, and abiding—is the best definition yet of what true spiritual worship consists of. When we sense the great love God has for us, when we gain security in our personal salvation, and when we find victory over our plaguing sins, our response is not only love for God but also our brothers and sisters in Christ and for lost sinners. "We love because He first loved us" (1 John 4:19). We will reach out in service because we desire to please God, but also because we realize His love for all humanity and long to serve them, too. Service will be the fruit of our worship.

Summary

In order for us to worship God in spirit and in truth, our lifestyle must bring glory to God. God is calling us to warfare against our inherited and cultivated tendencies. He is giving us the opportunity to gain battle experience in calm and peaceful times, to prepare for the trying times ahead. The Bible presents five warfare tactics:

1. *Submission to God.* It prepares us for the rest of the war. Without submission we have no power to resist evil. When we submit to God, He puts His armor upon us (Eph. 6:10-18), and His armor protects us from the enemy.

2. *Resist the devil.* God promises that if we resist Satan, he will flee from us (James 4:7-10; 1 Peter 5:8, 9). Ways to resist the devil: quote Scripture, pray, praise God aloud in song or spoken word, and make a verbal confession of faith in Jesus.

3. *Flee from idolatry* (1 Cor. 10:14). Look for the way of escape (verse 13).

4. *Obey God and keep His commandments.* Obedience to God's commands puts a hedge around the Christian that Satan cannot penetrate.

5. *Watch and pray* (Matt. 26:41). Jesus should be the most important part of our life. Every day we need to pray and make sure that our lives conform to His life. We need to carefully guard our thoughts so that we do not store up grievances and resentments. And we should not passively cover them up, but aggressively give them over to Jesus.

As we learn God's warfare tactics we will find a change in our lifestyle, a new depth to our worship.

CHAPTER 4

Worthy of Worship

George was the least likely divinity student at the University of Halle, no matter that the Lutheran state church of Germany had accepted him. Instead of spending his time in serious study and preparation for a pastorate, George wasted a good many hours at the village tavern drinking beer and having a good time with his friends. Amid roars of laughter his fellows described him as the "only divinity student who pawns his watch to pay his card debts more often than he reads his Bible." As far as anyone could tell, George had not the slightest leaning toward God.

George had signed up as a divinity student because his father had decided that the best way to make sure of a good future for his son was to find him a place with the state church in which the pay was good, and once he was accepted, the job would be for life. No matter that George did not attend church and did not even believe in God. One must be prudent in looking to the future.

His friends included another unlikely individual. He was a small, timid chap who had gone to school with George in his hometown when they were just boys. George had been the popular one, always laughing and at the center of any mischief. Beta, the small fellow, had been shy and awkward. With a Bible under his arm, he was often hurrying to a Bible study, slowing down only to berate George about his evil ways.

When they first met at the university, George didn't recognize him until Beta brought up the past.

"I've always admired you, George," he said. "You always seem to be having such a good time. I've decided I'd like to try living like you do."

George stared in unbelief at the young man. *Oh, well*—he shrugged his shoulders—*let him try.*

Soon Beta was drinking along with the best of them and was one of George's intimate friends. "There's a place I'd like you to go with me this Wednesday," Beta said to George one day.

"A new tavern?" George asked.

"No, not that," Beta stammered. "You see, although I go drinking with you, I haven't completely given up on God. I'd like you to go to a prayer meeting with me. I attend every Wednesday night at a friend's house."

George chortled. "Prayer meeting?" he gasped. "But home meetings are against the law."

"Oh, nobody preaches," Beta explained. "They just sing, read a sermon, and pray."

Suddenly the adventure of attending an illegal prayer meeting caught George's fancy.

"Fine," he agreed. "I'll meet you here at the tavern, and we'll go on together. Maybe it will be good fun."

The next evening a nervous Beta led George to a house in the center of a row of stone houses, in which the Christians already gathered greeted them warmly.

"Happy to have you here, brothers," Beta's friend told the two university students. He led George to a small stool in the inner circle of a group of chairs. George glanced around at the sturdy-looking older men in attendance. Not a man had the ascetic appearance of a saint. Yet these men dared to defy the law and meet at home to worship their God.

One man, whom the others familiarly addressed as brother, offered prayer. George watched him, expecting him to stand for prayer as did those who prayed in the state churches. Instead, the man slid from his seat to his knees and began to pray as though he was talking to Someone of power who was right in the room with them, Someone so close that the speaker felt it necessary to respond to Him in a physical way.

George had never seen a man kneel to pray before. The thought came to him that if God really did exist, that would be the way He should be addressed. He turned to Beta and asked why the man knelt.

"That's the way it's always done," his friend whispered.

"Why?" George persisted.

"I don't know why," Beta responded. "But that's the way they always pray."

"Not where I've been," George muttered. "I'll tell you why the man knelt," he said thoughtfully, answering his own question as the two young men left the meeting. "The man knelt because he wanted to tell God that he was humble and human and that God was all-powerful and all-wise.

"He was showing his awe, his fear, his adoration, Beta!" George spoke with a solemn earnestness unusual to him. "What a man he must be to do that! And what a God he must worship!"

George was never the same after that evening. When he arrived home he went straight to his bedroom, threw off his coat, and dropped to the floor on his knees.

When you kneel like this, low before the Highest One, meekly before the Omnipotent One, George thought, *then God is real.* He who had not thought he believed in God now burst into prayer. "At last! God, tonight I am Yours!"

George Mueller had found a God worthy of worship, a God before whom men knelt in prayer.

I discovered this little-known story of George Mueller's conversion in a small biography by Faith Coxe Bailey (Chicago: Moody Press, 1958). Although I have read many biographies of the man who became known for his great faith as he trusted God to provide for the countless orphans he housed and cared for, I had never heard an account of his conversion before. And it has impressed me as much as Mueller was impressed by the man who knelt to pray. If only I could pray like that! If only God could use my public prayers to convert a soul! If only I could worship like that!

Should all God's people pray like that, what a power it would unleash in the world! The presence of God would fill the whole earth.

I doubt that any special posture earns merit with God. But the contrast of a man upon his knees in humility to pray before God drew George Mueller to the realization that God really did exist. Expressing our humility and awe before God in physical ways has power to make God real to us and to those around us, whether it be kneeling in submission, raising our hands in supplication, singing in praise or adoration, standing in honor and respect, merely bowing our heads in humility and reverence, or removing our shoes at His divine command.

The Hebrew priest who understood the symbols of the sanctuary, humbly and reverently took care of the daily needs of the house of God, and faithfully served the people touched the lives of those for whom he officiated. A worshiping heart does not go unnoticed either by the great God of the universe or by the people seeking Him.

Recently I returned from a camp meeting at which the evening speaker, the head of the Religion Department of a Christian college, felt himself so moved by the message he was presenting that he would sometimes stop and exclaim, "I love it! I love it!" The audience responded with warmth. We too loved it! Each of us sensed God's presence in the meeting. Not only was this man worshiping God, he was leading us to worship.

When Christians present a God worthy of worship before the world, thousands hungering for just such a God will respond just as George Mueller did. The warmth of a worshiping heart is contagious.

Moses learned to worship in the stillness of the desert as he herded sheep. In his youth he had been sure of his calling as

God's choice to deliver a whole nation from the powerful grip of Egypt. He could clearly see God's hand in his adoption into the very family of Pharaoh, the guidance and teaching of his slave birth parents in his early youth, his extensive education in the best schools of Egypt, and his experience in the armies of Pharaoh. The young would-be deliverer was ready for his destiny.

But his ambitious plans failed to materialize, and he found himself a wanderer, far from Egypt, with his only army a herd of sheep. The aging shepherd was hardly recognizable as the fiery young zealot of his Egyptian days. His quick mind had slowed to the pace of his sheep. Guiding his flock to food and water and finding a safe shelter for them at night were his sole concerns. With old age had come patience and tolerance. He had married and now had sons of his own. When he thought of the past, it was only to dream.

If God had really called him to lead the Hebrews to freedom, he had surely bungled it, he decided. Yet even now, as he herded the sheep, it seemed to him that circumstances pointed to His call having been a true one. Surely it was God who had saved his life as a child and equipped him for war and leadership in the household of Pharaoh. He deeply regretted the impetuousness of his youth, but realized he could not turn back the pages of his life. Now he was old and content to commune with God as he cared for his sheep, to teach his sons the lessons he had learned the hard way, to remind them again and again that God had made an everlasting covenant with their father Abraham that one day they would be a vast people.

And yet he alone of his people had escaped slavery in Egypt. The rest of the children of Abraham were weary slaves to an idolatrous nation, not even allowed to worship the true God. Surely God must have an alternate plan for the Israelites, since he—Moses—had thwarted His original purpose.

One day as he was searching for better pasture for his sheep in the desert, he noticed a bush on fire, although he had seen no lightning that could have ignited it. His first thought, of course, was for the protection of his flock. If the fire should spread, he would need to find safety for his flock. But as he watched intently, the bush did not burn up and the fire did not reach out to surrounding vegetation.

"This is strange," Moses mused. "I'll take a closer look." And he approached it.

"Moses, Moses," a voice called to him from within the fire.

In awe, Moses responded, "Here I am."

"Do not come any closer," the voice said. "Take off your sandals, for the place where you are standing is holy ground" (Ex. 3:4, 5).

Stooping, Moses removed his sandals, shaking a little as he realized that he had heard the voice of God. Did God still have a purpose for his life? What did God want with an old shepherd?

"I am the God of your father, the God of Abraham, the God of Isaac and the God of Jacob" (verse 6). Moses not only stood barefoot before the bush but hid his face as well. Who was he to look at God?

God went on to tell Moses that He had seen the misery of the people He had chosen to be His special people, who were now slaves in Egypt.

"I am concerned about their suffering," God said, "and so I have come down to rescue them from the Egyptians and to bring them out of that land into a goodly land flowing with milk and honey." As God went on to describe the land He had chosen for His people, Moses realized that although it was a country inhabited now by fierce and warlike people, it was the very land God had originally promised to Abraham. God had not given up on His original plan!

The Lord's next words surprised Moses.

"So now, go. I am sending *you* to Pharaoh to bring my people the Israelites out of Egypt" (verse 10).

The man sputtered in amazement. "Me? Not me, Lord. I'm only a shepherd. Who am I to be a leader?"

"Moses, Moses," God must have chided, "I prepared you

for this work years ago. But just to make you feel a little more confident, I'll give you a sign that I am sending you to do this. When you have brought the people out of Egypt, you will bring them to the place you are now, and here you will all worship Me."

The rest of how Moses protested and God persisted appears in Exodus 3-7. How amazed Moses must have been to find that although years had passed—wasted years, to his mind—God's original plan for the rescue of His people was still in force. The call Moses had received in his youth was still valid.

When Moses finally stood with the multitude of ex-slaves in the desert around Mount Sinai and learned with the people God's plans for worship, when he heard God's powerful voice proclaiming the Ten Commandments from the cloud surrounding the mountaintop, his heart must have reached out in awe and reverence to a God who could complete a plan like that. As the plan unfolded more and more, and the artisans completed the sanctuary—and as Moses caught a glimpse of the magnitude of God's plan for the entire race of humanity—he must have been grateful that God had not forgotten the lonely tired shepherd in the desert. The Bible says of Moses: "The Lord would speak to Moses face to face, as a man speaks with his friend" (Ex. 33:11).

Moses had learned how to worship God in spirit and in truth. He had found a God worthy of worship.

It is up to you and me to reveal to the world the worth of our Creator. Revelation 14 describes this final depiction of God's worth as the proclamation of angels. Although given by human voices, angelic power will accompany it, and it reaches everyone who lives upon earth. It is a message of worship. "Fear God and give him glory, because the hour of his judgment has come. Worship him who made the heavens, the earth, the sea and the springs of water" (Rev. 14:7).

In John the revelator's view of heaven, myriads of heavenly beings pronounced in song that Jesus is worthy of worship:

"You are worthy to take the scroll and to open its seals,
    because you were slain,
and with your blood you
    purchased men for God
from every tribe and language
    and people and nation.
You have made them to be a kingdom and priests
to serve our God,
and they will reign on the earth" (Rev. 5:9, 10).

As John watched the heavenly scene he saw hundreds of thousands of angels around the throne of God, plus four living creatures and 24 elders. This group continued singing:

"Worthy is the Lamb, who was slain,
    to receive power and wealth
    and wisdom and strength
    and honor and glory and praise!" (verse 12).

Then the song of praise swelled as every creature in heaven and on earth and on the sea joined in:

"To him who sits on the throne
    and to the Lamb
be praise and honor and glory
    and power,
    for ever and ever!" (verse 13).

One day we too will stand in heaven upon a place John the revelator portrayed as a sea of glass. We will be a multitude more numerous than the Israelites, and we will sing with glorified voices the song of Moses and the Lamb, worshiping God in the fullness of our redemption. And we will talk with Him face-to-face.

But could it be possible that we need not wait to know the

glories of heaven before we fully worship God? Could whole-hearted worship by His chosen last-day people be God's chosen means of lighting up the earth with His glory?

> " 'No eye has seen,
>   no ear has heard,
>   no mind has conceived
>   what God has prepared for those
>   who love him'—
>   but God *has revealed* it to us by his Spirit"
>   (1 Cor. 2:9, 10).

We often apply this verse to the future, but I believe God is talking about the possibilities He has in mind for us right now. If we could open our minds to God's greatness and power, might it not be possible that we could join the angels, the four living creatures, and the 24 elders right now in singing that chorus of worship? Could it be that when we reach out daily to worship God in spirit and in truth our voices reach around the world proclaiming that the God of heaven is worthy of worship? Can we perhaps be a part of that mighty angelic cry to worship God here and now?

It is not in heaven or some future day. Now is the time to light up the world with our worship.

He is a God worthy of our worship.

Summary
When Christians present a God worthy of worship before the world, thousands who hunger for just such a God will respond by yielding their lives to Him.

God can use only people who have learned to worship.

Moses worshiped God in the quietness of the desert, herding sheep. The Lord met him at the burning bush and called him to the front line of the battle. The Hebrew deliverer had found a God worthy of worship, a God he could follow in service.

It's up to you and me to reveal to the world the worth of our Creator. The last message God has for the world is a message of worship: "Fear God and give him glory, because the hour of his judgment has come. Worship him who made the heavens, the earth, the sea and the springs of water" (Rev. 14:7).

While this message is to be given by human voices, the power of an angel will accompany it. Meanwhile, in heaven thousands of angels, plus the four living creatures and the 24 elders, join in singing:

> "Worthy is the Lamb, who was slain,
>   to receive power and wealth
>   and wisdom and strength
>   and honor and glory and praise!" (Rev. 5:12).

Then all creatures in heaven and earth add their voices in singing:

> "To him who sits on the throne
>   and to the Lamb
>   be praise and honor and glory
>   and power,
>   for ever and ever!" (verse 13).

We can join in that chorus even now as we worship God in spirit and in truth. Our worship will light up the whole world with God's glory. Each of us can proclaim from one end of the earth to the other that the God who created the heavens and the earth and everything in it is a *God worthy of worship.*

CHAPTER 5

Holy Spirit, Guide in Worship

The Holy Spirit enjoys nothing so much as leading human beings into worship of the heavenly Father and adoration of the Son. But sadly, humanity seldom follows the Spirit's prompting toward worship.

We may seek Him eagerly for victory over sin, for personal gifts, even for instruction, but we rarely follow His direction in worship. So often we respond with fear, indifference, or carelessness to the Holy Spirit's call to worship.

Early on in my prayer walk, back in the days when I began intensely seeking Him for intimacy, the Spirit began inviting me to a deeper worship. I cherished the way the Holy Spirit taught me, I reveled in the joy and peace He brought me, but I ran away when the Spirit urged me beyond my comfort zone in worship. One early evening I was kneeling beside my bed in prayer, called there by the Spirit to pray at a time I did not usually do so, when the Spirit overwhelmed me with His power and glory. I didn't know what to do with such intensity. Frightened, I arose from my knees and joined my children in the family room watching television. I traded an adventure in worship for watching *Ironside* on TV!

Along with this memory comes others as I realize that I often treat the Holy Spirit casually when He woos me to worship. Although I am no longer afraid when I sense His extraordinary presence in my life, yet unless it is during my planned prayer time, I tend to enjoy His presence passively, without responding in praise and thanksgiving. In speaking of times of special Spirit outpouring, Ellen White says, "The Lord tested you, to see if you would treat His rich blessing as a cheap, light matter, or regard it as *a rich treasure* to be handled with *reverent awe*" (*Selected Messages,* book 1, p. 139; italics supplied).

The Holy Spirit is a "rich treasure to be handled with reverent awe"! How often have I failed to treat Him as such. So often I have rejoiced in the spiritual blessing, yet failed to regard His presence as a precious gift. It's almost as though I regard Him as a servant and His presence as something I deserve. And of course, when I do that I miss the grace God sought to give me. Ellen White continues in the same passage I have quoted above, saying that when we receive the presence of the Holy Spirit as a treasure, God will double the grace He gives us just as He did the talents of the man in the New Testament story who faithfully handled what his master had given him. Oh, how I need doubled grace!

The Holy Spirit never comes for our personal pleasure, but only so we can grow in intimacy with God and thus glorify Him in ministry, praise, and worship. Our response to the presence of the Holy Spirit in our hearts should always be praise, thanksgiving, and worship. God will reveal to us the appropriate vehicle for this expression as we open ourselves fully to His infilling.

As I searched for a suitable personal example to share with you, one that will help you recognize such moments in your own life and yet not bare something meant to be kept just between the Lord and me, I've found that the Holy Spirit's intervention in my life is so varied that it may not be possible to use only one illustration. In *Sensing His Presence, Hearing His Voice* I tell of the six-week period when the Holy Spirit taught me about spiritual housekeeping, using my daily housework as a teaching tool for spiritual lessons. What I was learning excited me, yet I took for granted that I would always have this daily, almost visible presence of God in my life. I did not treat Him as a rich treasure. My life is still blessed from that period of teaching by God, yet I am certain that I missed the double blessing promised by not handling the gift with reverent awe. The amazing thing about God is that He understands our human frailties and blesses us nevertheless—though we may miss the *full* blessing possible.

God has not promised that Christians will be supercharged with the power of the Holy Spirit in a noticeable way at all times, but He does assure us that we can walk continually in the power of the Spirit. The Bible tells us that He is with us just as surely in the dark times as in the light. But we must always be ready to respond to the unleashing of His power in us and be eager to take advantage of the opportunities He opens before us, either for witnessing or for worship. The call of the Holy Spirit to worship is a summons to meet God and to hear what He has to say, and an opportunity for us to offer praise to Him.

Sometimes the call to special worship arrives during my regular prayer times and manifests itself by great freedom and joy in my prayer; sometimes tears, songs of joy, many smiles, and a feeling of great closeness to the Lord. I love those times.

Occasionally the divine invitation comes at an unusual time and consists mainly of a sense of the glory of the Lord flowing over me, through me, and around me. I just sit back and enjoy His presence, praising Him aloud if I am alone, and thanking Him.

I realize that God works through our individual personalities, and so God's call to worship may differ widely with each of you. Because of my excitement with discovering God's willingness to draw closer and closer to me in an intimate relationship, I may sound as though I think each of you must have exactly the experience that I have with God in order for it to be genuine. But I don't *really* think that way. I know that God works with each of us in just the way that is best for us. A lovely Christian woman I know says that although she has a deep confidence that God is leading her—through her Bible study and in daily providences—yet she is never conscious of actually hearing the voice of God. (It is the same woman who asked me what daydreaming is! Perhaps God can lead her in a much more straightforward path than He can me because of her very practical mind. My own mother has told me much the same thing, and I know she walks closely with God.)

I do know that more and more God is inviting His people to special times of intimate worship—people have told me so. One woman I know finds such times of worship as she meditates in her prayer garden. Some encounter it as they walk. We need to deliberately give God opportunities to commune with us by planning pauses in the midst of our activities. However, sometimes I have found God willing to run right along with me in my rush and whisper in my ears all the while. He or she who has spiritual ears will hear!

A very different story of a surprise visit by the Holy Spirit happened during my days as an academy librarian.

The student body assembly was in an uproar over the issue of school banquets. Students sat in orderly rows in the gym, interspersed randomly with faculty members. The missing principal had sent a letter to the student body via the student body president. The gist of the letter was that the students could have no more banquets.

As the student association president read the letter, I knew why the principal had written it. The faculty had sat in long and serious discussion on the subject. Our students were used to elegant banquets catered in nice restaurants with expensive entertainment after the meal. Because student enrollment was down this year, school finances could not supplement the money received from the tickets sold. It was the consensus of the faculty that a change was necessary. But I had never dreamed that the principal would choose this way of communicating our decision.

The rumble in the gym became louder as student after student voiced indignation. They resented the fact that the principal had written a letter while sitting in the seclusion of his office rather than facing them in person. They decided that the faculty and the church—and maybe even God—didn't want them to have a good time.

Rarely did a teacher speak out in town hall meetings. It was a time primarily for student expression. Even more surely I, the librarian, had never even harbored the thought of speaking up in a town hall meeting! But today I wished that someone, student or teacher, would add a word of sanity to the rising mob spirit. I felt that God especially was being misrepresented.

The next thing I knew I was standing in the aisle holding a microphone in my hand, although I had no memory of making a decision to speak, of rising, or of stepping out into the aisle. But there I stood!

"Students," I began, "God loves banquets. He has invited all of you to the most glorious banquet ever planned." And I went on to tell about the great banquet Jesus will hold for the redeemed.

The noise in the gym subsided. I took my seat, and the student body president went on to other business. The meeting adjourned quietly, and subdued students went back to classes.

The interesting thing to me was that *no one,* either faculty or student, ever mentioned to me my uncharacteristic speech in town hall. It was as though it had never taken place. But the effect remained. I heard no more of the rebellion against the school ruling against restaurant banquets. Other plans went into effect. The academy students attended banquets held in the nearby church fellowship hall. Parents and faculty members cooked the meals, and volunteers provided entertainment.

Often I have marveled at the smoothness of the solution. Why did I speak out? Who put those words in my mouth? Usually I avoid confrontation at all costs.

I feel certain that the Holy Spirit used me as an instrument that day. I spoke with Holy Spirit power. That speech was my appropriate response to His presence in my life. How thankful I am that I responded!

The Bible records numerous thrilling examples of the Holy Spirit's invitation to worship. Perhaps my favorite is the call of the young Isaiah to join in worship before the throne of God in vision. As the angels called, "Holy, holy, holy is the Lord of hosts" around the glorious throne, and the smoke of God's consuming fire filled the Temple till the doorposts and the thresholds shook, Isaiah recognized his unfitness for God's presence.

"I'm unclean," he cried, "and I've seen the King, the God of heaven. I shouldn't be here! Woe is me!"

Immediately God sent an angel with a live coal from the altar to touch Isaiah's mouth.

"See," encouraged the angel, "this has touched your lips; your guilt is atoned for."

At that moment the enraptured Isaiah heard the voice of God Himself asking, "Whom shall I send? Who will speak for Us?"

Eagerly the prophet responded, "I'm here! Send me!"

"Go," God said. "I am sending you to speak to My people for me."

The summons to worship by the Holy Spirit is an opportunity for preparation for service.

The little boy Samuel encountered the power of the Holy Spirit when God called him during the night, and thus he began a long life of worship and service.

God Himself touched the mouth of the young Jeremiah, saying, "Now, I have put my words in your mouth . . . I appoint you over the nations and kingdoms" (Jer. 1:9, 10).

Obviously God does not call all of us as prophets, but He summons us all to service, and we can be fitted for our work only through the power of the Holy Spirit in personal worship.

How will God choose to reveal Himself in these last days? Will He use the same ways He employed in Bible times, or will He devise new methods? Do we limit Him by our fear and our unbelief?

I know one thing—I want to be a part of the action, whatever it is. I desire to be wholly open to the Holy Spirit in my own life, and I long to worship Him with all my heart. When the days of persecution come and the saints walk with the light of heaven shining directly upon them with angels accompanying them (see *Testimonies,* vol. 9, p. 16), I want to be one of those saints!

I often hear the words "conservative" and "liberal" bandied about as though we have to make a choice between the two in our Adventism. My husband and I had always considered ourselves conservative Adventists until we moved from a church that leaned toward what some referred to as "new theology" to an ultraconservative church. We looked forward eagerly to a united church board. What a surprise to find that the new congregation had a liberal element too, and it was my husband and me! Our views that our former congregation had tagged "conservative" the new church considered "liberal"!

I prefer not to use these terms in describing myself or my church. Oh, yes, I long to be liberal in giving, in loving, in forgiving, in hospitality, and in spreading the gospel. And I desire to be conservative in lifestyle. But I want to be *zealous,* rather than conservative, in my approach to the gospel and witnessing. Although I hold fast to the truths given us in the past, I wish to be open to new applications of truth, to new ways of worship, both in private and in groups. And I seek to be flexible, rather than stiff, in dealing with others. I support my church leadership with my prayers and my money, knowing that they are not perfect and that sometimes my money may be used improperly. Not that I condone intolerance or politics in leadership—we should never passively accept ineptness or rigidity. I am vocal in supporting the need for change and will do what I can to transform things around me. But I refuse to be drawn into arguments or criticism. Instead, I pledge myself to intercession for revival and reformation for my denomination, praying for specific individuals and situations, trusting that God Himself will work the change.

I look to the future with eager expectancy. There exists no

limit to what God can accomplish through a repentant, praying people. I like the words *zealous, courageous, fearless,* and *passion.* Thus I want to be zealous in witnessing, courageous in the face of opposition, and fearless even when confronted with disapproval. Jesus told the people that the kingdom of heaven began advancing forcefully through the preaching of John the Baptist, and since that time "forceful men lay hold of it" (Matt. 11:13). That doesn't sound very conservative to me! I want to be forceful in my love for God, passionate in my witnessing. I want to praise God openly and often. I want to respond to the moving of the Holy Spirit in my life with worship and praise in the way the Spirit leads. I want to speak up when He gives me words, I want to shout when He leads me to shout, sing when He urges me to sing, dance when He asks me to dance. And most of all, I want to pray when He calls me to prayer.

The Holy Spirit is calling us today as a church as well as individually to put away all hardness of heart toward our leadership, toward God, toward each other, and toward sinners. We must dig out the roots of bitterness and dissension. God can not bless us with the fullness of the Holy Spirit in our gatherings until we individually do this work of repentance and confession. It is our call to worship.

The sanctuary shows us the work of the Holy Spirit in worship. Just within the curtains of the holy place stood a golden candlestick with seven lamps lit with holy fire and kept continually burning. Olive oil, representing the Holy Spirit, fueled them. The lampstand symbolized God's people, His church—you and me (see Rev. 1)—through whom the holy oil must flow.

The Bible gives us three lists concerning the Holy Spirit and His role in our lives. In the first list the prophet Isaiah (Isa. 11:1-5) shared the ways the Holy Spirit would work in the life of the Son of God when He became a man to protect Him from temptation and to empower Him for service. I discussed this passage more fully in chapter 2. God promises each of us this very same power for victory and service in our daily lives.

The apostle Paul tells us in the second list how the Spirit will reveal Himself in the lives of Spirit-filled Christians, the fruit that they will exhibit (Gal. 5:22, 23). Charles Stanley, in his book *The Wonderful Spirit-filled Life* (Thomas Nelson, 1995), describes the importance of this fruit. He says that the evidence of fruit in the lives of believers fills three important functions in the church:

1. The fruit attracts non-Christians to the church. When Christians reveal love, joy, peace, patience, kindness, goodness, faithfulness, gentleness, and self-control in their daily lives, it is a fragrance that attracts others to Jesus.

2. The fruit is like oil to keep the church running without friction. Without the qualities of the fruit Christians cannot work together in harmony. It is the fruit that produces unity.

3. The fruit protects us individually from evil around us. How? Because the qualities Paul lists are Spirit-produced, not the product of our willpower or policy, they are not changeable. Based upon the person of Jesus, they lead to character that endures.

"Love—for those who do not love in return.

"Joy—in the midst of painful circumstances.

"Peace—when something you were counting on doesn't come through.

"Patience—when things aren't going fast enough for you.

"Kindness—toward those who treat you unkindly.

"Goodness—toward those who have been intentionally insensitive to you.

"Faithfulness—when friends have proved unfaithful.

"Gentleness—toward those who have handled you roughly.

"Self-control—in the midst of intense temptation" (*Stanley,* p. 108).

The olive oil that fueled the lamps of the sanctuary stands for the work of the Holy Spirit in our individual lives. The priests continually cleaned the lamps so the oil would flow freely. It is our responsibility to keep the channels of our minds open to the power of the Holy Spirit so that we can acceptably worship God and serve humanity.

The third list about the Holy Spirit occurs in Paul's descriptions of how God prepares the church for service (Rom. 12; 1 Cor. 12; Eph. 4). When God asked Moses to build Him a sanctuary that He might live among His people, He specifically gifted individuals with skills for the task. As He began His New Testament church He instructed Paul that He was gifting individuals to administer and serve in it. Every born-again Christian receives at least one gift for service. As we use them, they will multiply.

During the past few years it has become popular to encourage church members to discover their spiritual gifts. Church leaders hold numerous seminars around the country for that purpose. As valuable as it is to discover and use our spiritual gifts, there is something more important. We all know churches filled with gifted people who are unable to use their God-given gifts for the glory of God because they have not allowed the oil of the Holy Spirit to flow through their lives and produce the fruit of the Spirit. Without the fruit we cannot use the gifts, because of dissention. It is only as we gather as a group of Christians bearing much fruit that such gifts can build up the church. Harmony and unity are a result of visible fruit of the Spirit.

The Bible gives us another word picture for the Holy Spirit. He is the rain God sent upon Palestine to produce a harvest. In Palestine the rainy season begins with a fall period of rain to germinate the seed and make it sprout, take root, and grow, and it ends with spring showers to bring the crop to full maturity. The early fall rain, the continual showers throughout the rainy season, and the concluding spring rain were all necessary to produce a harvest. God promised both periods of heavier rain to the obedient people. When they fell into idol worship, God often withheld the rains.

The promised rain of the Holy Spirit watered the disciples

at Pentecost, causing the seed planted by Jesus to germinate and grow. That rain has been available to Christians in all ages. Showers have fallen upon God's people all through time. But now we are nearing the end of time, and we need the concluding latter rain, representing the spiritual grace that will prepare the church for the coming of Christ. Everything that has been planted must reach full maturity before Jesus returns again.

The latter rain will not benefit anyone who has not received the former rain. Unless we repent of our hardness of heart, of our inhumanity to others, of our self-righteousness and pride, as well as our impurity and idolatry, we will not experience the latter rain.

"Only those who are living up to the light they have will receive greater light. Unless we are daily advancing in the exemplification of the active Christian virtues, we shall not recognize the manifestations of the Holy Spirit in the latter rain. It may be falling on hearts all around us, but we shall not discern or receive it" *(Testimonies to Ministers,* p. 507).

"Divine grace is needed at the beginning, divine grace at every step of advance, and divine grace alone can complete the work. . . . A connection with the divine agency every moment is essential to our progress. We may have had a measure of the Spirit of God, but by prayer and faith we are continually to seek more of the Spirit. It will never do to cease our efforts. If we do not progress, if we do not place ourselves in an attitude to receive both the former and the latter rain, we shall lose our souls, and the responsibility will lie at our own door" *(ibid.,* p. 508).

Ellen White says in another place that "the convocations of the church, as in camp meetings, the assemblies of the home church, and all occasions where there is personal labor for souls, are God's appointed opportunities for giving the early and the latter rain" *(ibid.,* p. 508).

I can remember so clearly the first time I read that passage. Oh, how I longed for the fullness of the Holy Spirit! I so feared missing out on the latter rain that I carefully gathered my little family together each Wednesday night and hurried them off to prayer meeting, although few other children attended midweek service and I received some negative comments from church members about subjecting my children to adult prayer meetings. Yet I am still glad today that I exposed them early to the fervent prayers, testimonies, and singing of those old-fashioned prayer meetings. If perchance someone in our family was sick and I had to miss the meeting, I always greeted my husband on his return home with an eager question: "Was the Holy Spirit poured out in latter-rain power on the prayer meeting tonight?"

One prayer meeting night we gathered together at the church with sorrowful hearts, for my husband had conducted the funeral that afternoon for the wife of one of our elders. She was an elderly woman who had been sick for quite a long time. I had never met her, for we were new to the congregation and she did not welcome company. But one member of our family had always been welcome in her home. My children took care of the church grounds to earn money to pay for their piano lessons. Elder Grant (not his real name) and his wife lived in a mobile home in a small trailer park just off the church property. My second son, Paul, about 10, had become special friends with the man, and he, in turn, had taken Paul in to meet his wife. Paul and Mrs. Grant had hit it off right from the start. Only a week or two before she died, Paul had given Mrs. Grant a Mother's Day corsage.

"She had me pin it onto her jacket," the boy told me delightedly.

The children had attended the funeral with me that afternoon, and they were very solemn this evening. As we were singing, I heard someone enter the chapel. Paul looked back to see who it was.

"Mom," Paul whispered to me, "Elder Grant just came in. Oh, he must be so lonely without his wife. May I go back and sit with him?"

I nodded my head, then turned and watched as the small

boy snuggled up close to the elderly man in the back pew.

Prayer time began, and many prayed for the lonely old man. I was surprised to hear my son's voice as for the first time he prayed in a public prayer meeting. He asked God to be very close to Elder Grant and not let him cry too much or be too sad. "Send Your angels to keep him company," pleaded my small son.

I don't suppose you could say that the Holy Spirit was there that night in latter-rain power, but I went home that evening knowing that Jesus Himself had been among us.

As the years passed by, I lost my urgency about the latter rain. I also discovered the story in the Old Testament of the 70 elders whom Moses called together for a special meeting. God put His Spirit upon each of those men and they prophesied. However, two of the elders did not attend the meeting at the tent—Scripture doesn't tell us why—yet God poured His Spirit upon them in their own tents, and they also began prophesying (Num. 11). After reading that story, I decided that if I should for some reason be unable to attend a meeting where the Holy Spirit poured Himself out in a special way, surely the Lord, knowing my eagerness for the latter rain, would put His Spirit upon me even at home!

Yet special blessings do attend those who gather together as brothers and sisters in Christ in prayer for His Spirit. Someday God will choose those meetings to pour out the Holy Spirit in latter-rain power for the closing of His work.

"Let us, with contrite hearts, pray most earnestly that now, in the time of the latter rain, the showers of grace may fall upon us. At every meeting we attend our prayers should ascend, that at this very time God will impart warmth and moisture to our souls. As we seek God for the Holy Spirit, it will work in us meekness, humbleness of mind, a conscious dependence upon God for the perfecting latter rain. If we pray for the blessing in faith, we shall receive it as God has promised" (*Testimonies to Ministers,* p. 509).

Worship is the human heart responding to the wooing of

the Holy Spirit. It is only as we learn to worship in spirit and in truth that God will be able to prepare us to receive the perfecting latter rain, which will enable us to give the fullness of the last message, described in Revelation 18, that will light up the whole earth with the glory of God.

Summary

The Holy Spirit enjoys nothing so much as leading human beings into worship of the heavenly Father and adoration of the Son. But so often we ignore His promptings to worship.

More and more the Holy Spirit seeks to lead His people to special times of intimate worship. We need to learn how to respond in the way God desires. God never gives the Holy Spirit for our personal pleasure, but only so we can grow in intimacy with Him. When we open our hearts to the filling of the Holy Spirit, our response will be praise, thanksgiving, worship, and ministry, all to the glory of God the Father.

Ellen White tells us that when we receive the Holy Spirit as a "rich treasure" God will double the grace He gives us, just as the talents of the man in Christ's parable were doubled.

The Holy Spirit is summoning us today as a church as well as individually to put away all animosity toward our leadership, toward God, toward each other, and toward sinners. We must let Him root out our bitterness. God cannot bless us with the fullness of the Holy Spirit in our gatherings until we individually repent and confess. It is our call to worship.

The sanctuary illustration of the Holy Spirit is the lampstand. It represents the church—you and me—through which the holy oil of the Holy Spirit flows. The Bible gives us three lists about the role of the Holy Spirit in our lives:

1. In the first list the prophet Isaiah (Isa. 11:1-5) shows us the ways that God the Father and God the Holy Spirit worked in the life of Jesus, when He became a man, to protect Him from temptation. The Holy Spirit wants to do this same work in each of us.

2. The second list describes how the Holy Spirit will reveal Himself in Spirit-filled Christians—the fruit of the Spirit—recorded in Galatians 5:22, 23.

3. The third list contains the gifts that the Holy Spirit bestowed upon the church when He came in Pentecostal power (Rom. 12; 1 Cor. 12; Eph. 4). Each born-again Christian receives at least one gift for ministry and service. As we use them, they multiply.

All three lists clearly remind us that the Holy Spirit wants to work in our lives to lead us to worship and service.

The Bible gives us one more word picture for the Holy Spirit. He is the rain sent upon Palestine to produce a harvest. In Palestine it took two periods of rain in a single rainy season to ensure a bountiful harvest. The fall rains to germinate the seed, make it sprout, make it take root, and make it grow came at the beginning of the rainy season. The spring rains that fell at the end of the rainy season brought the crops to full maturity. It required both periods of rain to bring forth a harvest. And God promised both to His obedient people.

The promised rain of the Holy Spirit fell upon the disciples at Pentecost, causing the seed planted by Jesus to germinate and grow. That rain has been available to Christians in all ages. But now as we near the end of time we need the latter rain that represents the spiritual grace that will prepare the church for Christ's coming. Everything that has been planted must reach maturity before Jesus returns again.

Worship is the human heart responding to the wooing of the Holy Spirit. It is only as we learn to worship in spirit and in truth that God will be able to prepare us to receive the latter rain which will enable us to give the fullness of the last message, described in Revelation 18.

CHAPTER 6

Markers Along the Narrow Way

If worship is a heart response to the discovery of a God worthy of worship, why even talk about it? Won't it just automatically come about, and won't God teach us individually how to do it?

Life has few automatic responses. Even when I'm sincerely loved by someone, my love response is seldom something that happens without thought. Rather I must choose to return that love. God didn't make us robots, but intelligent creatures. The intelligent response of love is much more meaningful, even in a human relationship, than just a natural and uncontrollable reaction of love. The natural response may stumble when the object of that love ceases to meet our expectations or stands in the way of some cherished desire. But the deliberate choice to love need never fail.

Like everything else in the Spirit-filled life, worship needs cultivation in order to grow. God led the people He chose to be His witnesses in the world out of slavery and into the wilderness, where they would have the time and the opportunity to worship Him. He gave them a visual illustration of what worship is like, revealed Himself in the cloud by day and the fire by night, spoke His commandments aloud from Sinai, and provided them the opportunity day by day to worship Him through the sanctuary services, with Moses and the priests to explain and lead.

We each need to look for visual illustrations of how to worship. The one God set up in the wilderness for the Israelites is still an excellent teacher. When Isaiah, by vision, saw God, it was in the Most Holy Place, with all the angels singing, "Holy, holy, holy." Daniel viewed the beginning of the pre-Advent judgment as God's throne moved from the holy to the Most Holy Place. Zechariah witnessed Joshua the high priest standing before the angel of the Lord as Satan accused him. The apostle John saw God upon His throne and the closing judgments taking place. God used illustrations from the sanctuary to lead all of these prophets to worship as well as to provide instruction and direction for the people.

I am grateful for the truths God has shown me about the kingdom of heaven. But the more I learn, the more I realize how insignificant it all is against the vastness of God's knowledge. And I'm humbled as I realize how very little I really know.

Thus my natural reaction is to keep quiet about the few things I do know, thinking that because it is so little it can't possibly be important enough for me to tell anyone. I remember the prophets of the past, the riches displayed in the Bible, the great books written today by theologians and leaders. Why should I write and speak my little in the face of their much?

But God assures me that actually all any human being has is just a fragment, however much it may seem to us. And the tiny bit I have to share may be exactly the piece missing in the understanding of someone else, thus enabling him or her to grasp a fuller picture of God than he or she had ever seen before.

Because I'm a visual person I like to illustrate my ideas with mind pictures. My first attempt at a picture for my little bit was a jigsaw puzzle with missing pieces. I saw my little bit of knowledge as a missing piece in someone else's picture of God. But then I discovered an even clearer picture—the Christian walk, which Jesus described as the "narrow way." We all start out on this path when we are born again.

My husband and I took church groups backpacking in the

High Sierras for 15 summers. Sometimes we came to places where the trail seemed to disappear as we crossed steep rocky hillsides. Often it was a long hard search to find the right direction to take across the rock and locate the path again on the other side. It was a lot easier for us when someone traveling the way before us had taken the time to erect a small stone marker to show us the direction on the rock face and again at the place where the trail began again. The same thing happens in the Christian walk. When we have difficulty knowing where the trail is, God sends someone to share their little bit of knowledge or insight with us, and we suddenly see the path clearly ahead of us.

I used to assume that the path was exactly alike for each of us. Oh, I wasn't naive enough to think our experiences would all be alike, but I did conclude that the road to eternal life consisted of learning the same lessons in the same order. But I was wrong. Sometimes the little I need to make the path ahead of me plain is something that a very new Christian has to offer me; other times it is something that I can learn from someone who has had long experience in the Spirit-filled life. Or I can gain it from my non-Christian neighbor. Or even by remembering something I learned myself or experienced in the past. Sometimes it may be something that I suddenly realize that I should have learned in the past but because of my frailty the Lord lifted me over a place where my upbringing or my genetic legacy made it impossible for me to see a path before me. God gently placed me where the path was clearly visible ahead of me.

But God leaves no empty spots in our past life histories. He wants to fill in all those places He carried us over in the past. Bit by bit He sends someone to share with us their own little so that we can not only see the path ahead, but look back and see the place He has carried us over in the past. This is the way God fills in the valleys and levels the hills (Isa. 40:4) of our misunderstandings—our lack of education and discipline in the past, our present weaknesses—and opens up the future, making a plain path for our feet. And if we're willing to share these insights with others, our little may do the same for them in their Christian walk. This book is my little bit on worship.

Since true worship is the foundation of our walk with God, we must avoid rote worship. Isaiah reported God's dislike of any worship that does not involve the heart. "These people come near to me with their mouth and honor me with their lips, but their hearts are far from me. Their worship of me is made up only of rules taught by men" (Isa. 29:13).

Ezekiel records God's words to him about the same thing: "My people come to you, as they usually do, and sit before you to listen to your words, but they do not put them into practice. With their mouths they express devotion, but their hearts are greedy for unjust gain. Indeed, to them you are nothing more than one who sings love songs with a beautiful voice and plays an instrument well, for they hear your words but do not put them into practice" (Eze. 33:31, 32).

It is so easy to fall into patterns of worship. God sent a message through John the apostle to the last church on earth about this very problem. The church at Laodicea didn't even know that they had anything wrong with their worship, yet it nauseated God (Rev. 3:16). Because they faithfully followed the form of religion they felt rich and secure and did not even recognize their terrible deficiency. How often that is our experience!

Someone once asked me if I was advocating a return to all the Old Testament rituals since I stress the study of the sanctuary and using the daily work of the priests as a guide for prayer. Quickly I explained that nothing but a heart relationship with God has any meaning. But rituals are important in the Christian walk, or God would not have given them to us. Properly used, they act as reminders and illustrations of truth.

As human beings we do need reminders—even to worship. The morning and evening sacrifices in the courtyard of the sanctuary illustrate the importance of daily intimacy with God. It's as true today as it was in the days of the Israelites of old—we need to worship God at the beginning of our day and again at its close.

And we must understand the difference between false and true worship. God clearly delineates the difference in the Ten Commandments. We are never to revere foreign gods before the one true God or to make idols and worship them. We are to hold even the name of God in holy awe. He shows the importance of the one day each week that He set aside expressly for worship. The Lord tells us whom to worship: the Creator of the heavens and the earth. The last six commandments deal with lifestyle worship, showing how even our behavior can be a part of our worship.

The Bible gives us numerous examples of both true and false worship. Cain and Abel both brought sacrifices to offer before the gate at Eden. Both men built altars and carefully laid their offering upon them. Fire came down from heaven and consumed Abel's offering of a lamb, the mark of its acceptance by God, but Cain's fruit remained there throughout the day. Why was Cain's worship not acceptable while Abel's was?

God cannot accept any worship that does not point to the death of Jesus on the cross. Abel's sacrifice of a lamb was only a symbol of the death of Jesus, looking forward by faith. But Cain was unwilling to admit His need of a Saviour. Unless our worship today centers on the cross, looking backward by faith to Jesus' death, it is not true worship. And unless we are in submission to God we cannot worship in spirit and in truth.

The rich young ruler watched Jesus with the children as He blessed them, longing to be a child again and receive that blessing. He approached Jesus and asked what he must do to inherit eternal life. Jesus looked into his face and loved him. The Saviour gave him a test. "Sell everything you have and give to the poor. . . . Then come, follow me," He said. The young man "became very sad, because he was a man of great wealth" (Luke 18:22, 23). The only way to truly worship God is with a humble and contrite heart, willing to give up everything to follow Him.

Mary Magdalene is an example of a true worshiper. She spent her life's savings in one lavish act of worship, anointing the head and feet of Jesus with expensive ointment. Judas took offense. Had we been there, might we perhaps have joined him in feeling it was false worship?

Two men went up to the Temple to worship. One, a Pharisee, bragged on how good he was and asked God for not a thing. The other man, a tax collector, bowed his head in confession of sin and asked for mercy. Which man worshiped in spirit and truth? Jesus tells us that the tax collector went home justified.

Sometimes preconceived ideas affect our perception of true and false.

During the late 1960s manufacturers had just perfected authentic-looking plastic fruit—grapes and cherries, apples and oranges, pears, peaches, and berries. I loved the luscious look of that fruit and could imagine all sorts of interesting home decorating possibilities with it. About that time my husband and I received an invitation to a friend's supper party. As I waited my turn at the buffet table, the beauty of the table centerpiece— cherries by the dozens cascading over a three-tiered glass dish—intrigued me.

"Those cherries look so real," I marveled, but I walked right past the centerpiece because I was positive they had to be plastic. I heaped my plate with good food and found a spot to sit beside my husband. As I looked up from my plate I saw him putting a cherry in his mouth. I held my breath—*he thought they were real!* How would he react to a plastic cherry?

My husband chewed a bit, then swallowed.

"There's nothing like a fresh cherry," he gloated. "They're my favorite fruit."

I looked around in bewilderment. Nearly every plate held some of those cherries. I glanced toward the buffet table. The tiered glass centerpiece was empty.

Laughter and talk flowed around me as I sat contemplating my incredible mistake. Although I am extremely fond of cherries I had none on my plate. Why? Because I confused the true with the false.

I was still quiet as my husband and I left the party for home. Oh, yes, the other guests had teased me endlessly about the absence of cherries on my plate when they learned my misconception.

"So you don't like cherries anymore?" one person slyly asked. I smiled wanly.

"Been eating any plastic cherries?" another questioned innocently. I glared back.

I was ready to leave when my husband suggested that he still had a sermon to work on. Hand in hand we walked the half block home through the darkness and stillness.

"What's wrong?" he asked. "It's not like you to mind teasing. In fact, I think you usually enjoy being teased."

"I know," I laughed ruefully. "I always enjoy the give and take of teasing and being in the center of it." Then I was quiet again.

"It isn't the teasing, honey, that bothered me," I finally burst out. "It's how easy it is to be mistaken about something I thought I was sure of! What if we make a mistake about something really important? Something like thinking the outpouring of the Holy Spirit in revival is just another false revival? I don't want to miss the latter rain! I want to recognize the true and real when it comes along."

But of course, I don't want to eat any plastic cherries, either!

So how can we tell truth from error?

The only safe way is to maintain an intimate relationship with God, submitting daily to His leading. You can't fool me into thinking someone else is my husband or that my husband is someone else! I see him every day—I *know* who he is.

But Satan is extremely tricky. Because he knows that error cannot stand alone, he attaches it like a parasite to the tree of truth. Remember the tree of good and evil in the Garden of Eden? Satan is still sneaking up on us with the same blended error and truth (*The Seventh-day Adventist Bible Commentary*, Ellen G. White Comments, vol. 5, p. 1095).

"The track of truth lies close beside the track of error, and both tracks may seem to be one to minds which are not worked by the Holy Spirit, and which, therefore, are not quick to discern the difference between truth and error" (*Selected Messages,* book 1, p. 202).

Ellen White also tells us that "the mind that depends on others is certain, sooner or later, to be misled" (*Education,* p. 231). So we need to learn to think for ourselves, to study things through.

"The power to discriminate between right and wrong we can possess only through individual dependence upon God. Each for himself is to learn from Him through His Word. Our reasoning powers were given us for use, and God desires them to be exercised. 'Come now, and let us reason together' (Isa. 1:18), He invites us. In reliance upon Him we may have wisdom to 'refuse the evil, and choose the good' (Isa. 7:15; James 1:5)" (*ibid.*).

If we walk daily with God in wholehearted worship and obedience, He will protect us from error. Does that mean we will never be mistaken? No, as human beings we may sometimes come to wrong conclusions. But then God will patiently show us yet another marker that will lead us back to truth.

In my first book, *Practical Pointers to Personal Prayer,* I wrote one chapter called "Altars Along the Way." In it I talked about the markers God had given me to keep me on the straight and narrow way. They were experiences and lessons through which I had come to understand truth. Many of my altars were scriptures God had made personal for me or times God had spoken to me about something in particular. Of course, my altars were not on public view—except as I shared them with others. But God desired me to hang the memories of these experiences like pictures upon the walls of my heart. These markers keep me on the track of truth.

Each person needs to begin their own collection of altars or markers. You see, my markers aren't nearly as helpful for you as are your own.

"It is for our own benefit to keep every gift of God fresh in our memory. Thus faith is strengthened to claim and to receive more and more. There is greater encouragement for us in the least blessing we ourselves receive from God than in all the accounts we can read of the faith and experience of others. The soul that responds to the grace of God shall be like a watered garden. . . . Let us then remember the loving-kindness of the Lord, and the multitude of His tender mercies. Like the people of Israel, let us set up our stones of witness, and inscribe upon them the precious story of what God has wrought for us. And as we review His dealings with us in our pilgrimage, let us, out of hearts melted with gratitude, declare, 'What shall I render unto the Lord for all His benefits toward me? I will take the cup of salvation, and call upon the name of the Lord. I will pay my vows unto the Lord now in the presence of all His people' (Ps. 116:12-14)" *(The Desire of Ages,* p. 348).

What shall be our response to God's goodness?

Praise and worship. Both in our private exercises and as we meet with others. Worship not only is our private love tribute to God but also our means of witnessing to His glory.

Summary
Since God did not make us robots, but intelligent creatures, He desires us to deliberately choose to worship Him, rather than depending on our natural emotional response. Emotional responses to love or worship will fail, but deliberate choices need never do so.

We must cultivate worship in order for it to grow. Each of us needs to look for visual illustrations of how to worship. The visual object lesson God set up in the wilderness for the Israelites is still an excellent teacher. Throughout Scripture God uses illustrations from the sanctuary to teach His people and to lead them to worship.

Even the human being with the greatest understanding of spiritual truths has only a little compared with the vastness of God's knowledge. But God asks each of us to share our little with others because it may be exactly what is missing in their understanding of God and may enable them to grasp a fuller picture of God than they have ever seen before.

We can grasp this by envisioning the narrow way that Christ spoke of—the Christian walk that we all start out on when we are born again. Just as a hiking trail needs markers along the way to direct the hikers, so we need the markers of others who have gone before us. Our little bit of knowledge or insight may be the marker especially critical in the life choices of someone else.

Because we all acquire life's lessons in different order, we can learn from very new Christians, even from our non-Christian neighbor who has been open to God's leading in some part of his or her life. And we should be eager to learn from those with long experience in the Spirit-filled life. Often God will use something from our own past to mark the present way for us.

Since true worship is the foundation of our walk with God, we must avoid rote worship. In order to avoid being deceived by Satan's tricks we each need to think for ourselves, to study things through. If we walk daily with God in wholehearted worship and obedience, He will protect us from error. Even when we sometimes come to wrong conclusions God will not forsake us, but lead us once again to find truth.

Individually we need to begin collecting memories that will clearly mark the narrow way both ahead of us and behind us. It is God's plan to show us not only how He is leading us now but also how He has led us in the past, so that we clearly see the entire road to eternal life.

CHAPTER 7

Jesus, Name
Above Every Name

True worship must have a solid foundation. We can't base it upon our feelings—they are unreliable. Nor can we root it upon circumstances, because they are always changeable.

So what is true worship built upon?

The apostle Paul says, "For no one can lay any foundation other than the one already laid, which is Jesus Christ" (1 Cor. 3:11). Jesus, the mighty Rock, is the foundation of all true worship.

I mentioned in another chapter the difficulty I had with self-centered praise. It's so easy to focus my praise to God totally upon myself and the things He has done for me. When I began to understand more clearly the greatness and majesty of God I wanted very much to praise Him unselfishly, not centered upon myself, but upon His marvelous divine attributes. So I searched Scripture for a picture of this awesome God. I found Him in the book of Isaiah. The young prophet had received a vision of God on His majestic heavenly throne, surrounded by singing angels, that changed the direction of Isaiah's life (Isa. 6). Later Isaiah records God speaking to the Israelites from that same glorious spot in heaven.

> "For this is what the high and lofty One says—
> he who lives forever, whose name is holy:
> 'I live in a high and holy place,

but also with him who is contrite
   and lowly in spirit,
to revive the spirit of the lowly
   and to revive the heart of the contrite'"
(Isa. 57:15, 16).

I began praising this infinite, high, and lofty God, omnipotent and omnipresent, surrounded by myriads of angels singing "Holy, Holy, Holy"—a truly beautiful and biblically accurate picture of God. Surely it would solve my self-centered praise. But would you believe it? I found I still had a problem with praise!

My daydreaming mind had difficulty focusing on reality in prayer. (This is one reason that sanctuary prayer has been such a blessing to me—the imagery of the sanctuary keeps my mind clearly focused.) As I praised the high and lofty God I discovered that I couldn't be sure that it was *real praise* coming from my heart. My mental image of God was so ethereal that I felt like I was making it up! I've never seen an angel with wings, I've never seen a throne on the clouds of heaven, and I have never seen the shining glory of God. It all felt totally unreal, as if I was making up a new fantasy!

Isaiah's picture is a true and accurate picture of God, a God wholly worthy of our worship. But I needed more understanding of Him to make my praise real. God's solution to my problem was put into place more than 2,000 years ago! You see, He understood that human beings would have a problem visualizing Him. So He became a human being just like you and me! He began His human life as a baby and grew up just as we do. Instead of robes of light, He wore clothes like those of the people around Him. God slept and ate and drank just as they did. But all the time He was wholly God. Although He came first of all to save us from our sins, in doing that He also gave us a concrete and understandable picture of God. The disciples kept prodding Jesus to tell them what the Father was like, and His answer was always that if they saw Him, they also saw the

Father. He and the Father were just alike. Matthew, Mark, Luke, and John, in telling the story of Jesus, make God so real that I have no problem with fantasy. I can center in on Jesus, the Son of God, exalting the Father through Him, and know my praise is real.

I still visualize God on His throne, and I love to think of God the Father and God the Son sharing it throughout the pre-Advent judgment. But centering my praise on Jesus makes a relationship with God today, tomorrow, and for eternity a sure thing. It gives me confidence. I know I'm not just imagining being a part of the family of God. Human praise to God can never be wholly divorced from what He has done for us individually. After all, the cross is central to all worship and all praise, and Jesus died on the cross for *me.*

When we go through the wonderful list of the Hebrew Old Testament names for God that Garrie Williams compiled in his book *Give the Holy Spirit a Chance* (pp. 78-84) as a basis for our praise to the Father, we still put ourselves into the picture. He is *our* shepherd, *our* protector, *our* provider, the God who sees *us, our* victory banner, *our* healer.

Even in praise God wants it to be our personal response to His love. "In order to commune with God, we must have something to say to Him concerning our actual life" (*Steps to Christ,* p. 93). My first self-centered praise was like a baby's reaction to its mother's attention. Everything for the baby centers on itself. I'm so glad God is patient with us, even accepting our infant praise to His glory. But I want to grow up and worship Him fully in spirit and in truth.

From the time of my very first seeking after God, memorization of Scripture has been an important aid in my growing intimacy with Him. The psalm writer David says, "I have hidden your word in my heart that I might not sin against you" (Ps. 119:11). God often uses such stored verses to call me to worship.

A few weeks ago a phrase of Paul's writings that I had never memorized came into my mind along with a great desire to learn the whole passage. The conviction was so strong that I knew the verses would have special meaning for me:

> "Your attitude should be the same as that of
>   Christ Jesus:
>   who, being in very nature God,
>   did not consider equality with God something
>   to be grasped,
>   but made himself nothing,
>   taking the very nature of a servant,
>   being made in human likeness.
>   And being found in appearance as a man,
>   he humbled himself
>   and became obedient to death—
>   even death on a cross!
>   Therefore God exalted him to the highest place
>   and gave him the name that is above every
>   name,
>   that at the name of Jesus every knee should bow,
>   in heaven and on earth and under the earth,
>   and every tongue confess that Jesus Christ is Lord,
>   to the glory of God the Father" (Phil. 2:5-11).

I enjoyed memorizing the passage more than any other I have ever learned. Usually it takes me days to memorize just one verse by carefully going over it again and again. But it took me less than an hour following one morning prayer time to have the seven verses word perfect! And every time I repeat them I thrill at the grand climax—"At the name of Jesus every knee should bow, in heaven and on earth and under the earth, and every tongue confess that Jesus Christ is Lord, to the glory of God the Father."

A day or two later I found another passage that seemed to echo the same intensity, and I memorized it, too: "To him who is able to keep you from falling and to present you before his glorious presence without fault and with great joy—to the only God our Savior be glory, majesty, power and authority, through Jesus Christ our Lord, before all ages, now and forevermore! Amen" (Jude 24, 25).

One night not long after I had preserved the two passages in my memory, I awoke about 3:00 in the morning and couldn't go back to sleep—unusual for me. Tossing and turning, wide awake, I wondered if I should just get up. Then I remembered the verses I had just memorized and began repeating them again and again in my mind, praising God for His glory, majesty, power, and authority, and symbolically bowing at the name of Jesus, name above all names. I had a wonderful period of worship until my usual rising time. It made me smile all the rest of that day, and I still smile when I think about those glorious hours!

We need often to meditate on the great sacrifice that all of heaven made on our behalf. Even before the creation of our world the Godhead planned that God the Son would be the link between heaven and our new planet. God the Son was the Word that spoke creation into being. It was His hands that formed Adam and Eve from the dust of the ground. The entrance of sin brought mercy and justice into this relationship. The Son spoke the Ten Commandments on Sinai. In the fullness of God's timing He came to earth and was born of a virgin, lived a sinless life, took the entire history of human sin upon Himself, and died the death that we deserved. But He did not remain in the grave. God the Father called Him and took Him back to heaven, where the Son is still our representative, interceding daily for us individually, pleading His blood shed for us as our right to eternal life. The sinless human life that He lived gives us the power for victory over sin and to glorify Him in the world through our witness.

And God the Father, being a true father, loves Jesus even more for what He has done for us. No wonder we worship a God like that! God the Father loves to have us worship Jesus. Our worship of Jesus is to the glory of the entire Godhead. In fact, the only way we can fully worship God the Father or God the Holy Spirit is through knowing and worshiping God the Son.

Humanity always faces the danger of two extremes. Sometimes I become so comfortable with being in God's center of attention that I become complacent about my salvation. God has chosen me. Of course, He will save me. But then Satan attacks me with his accusations and I panic.

"How do I know I won't end up among the wicked?" I ask myself. "How can I be sure I have accepted Him and He has saved me?" Sometimes God's love seems far away like my nebulous God of worship. "How can I ever be sure of my salvation?"

I remember thinking about these very things when I was 7 or 8 years old. We often think that young children don't have deep thoughts about salvation, but that is far from true. One day I was entertaining myself in the living room with my small blackboard and a brand-new piece of white chalk, savoring the joy of drawing with a piece of chalk that no one had ever used before.

"Carrol," Mother called from the kitchen, "where are you?"

"Here, Mother, in the living room, drawing," I answered.

She came and stood beside me.

"What are you drawing?" she asked.

"Why, I'm drawing God," I answered. "See, this line is heaven and this is God's throne and this is God sitting on His throne."

Mother smiled as she examined my drawing, for I had copied my picture of God almost exactly from the king pictured on the box of White King laundry soap that Mother used. "What makes you think God looks like that?" she asked, trying to hide her smile.

"Well, God is a king, you know, and that's the way to draw kings. My favorite psalm, the twenty-fourth one, says He's the 'King of glory.'"

My mother seemed interested in her young daughter's ideas of God, so I continued.

"I really think God is especially fond of me because I'm sick so much and have to be alone a lot. I'm sure that no matter what I do, He'll save me a place right there." I made a chalk mark beside my King on the blackboard. Mother raised her eyebrows slightly at this bit of information.

"Carrol," Mother explained, "I'm sure God does give extra strength to those who are sick. But there will be no sinners in heaven even if they have been sick. Your sins will all have to be forgiven."

As I knelt for prayer with my sisters that evening I remembered Mother's words. Somehow I couldn't pray, for I was thinking about the one pet sin that I had convinced myself God would overlook in my case.

I loved to read and devoured anything that came into the house. I had even read my father's book on beekeeping! We had few books, but the neighbors often brought magazines for me to look through and cut up for scrapbooks, since asthma prevented me from attending school. Because I was still so young, no one, including my mother, dreamed that I read the adult stories from *The Country Gentleman, Ladies' Home Journal,* and other magazines of that day. In fact, since I had not been to school, no one had really taught me how to read. I had discovered it all on my own by observing Mother and Daddy and asking questions, especially of my older sister when she came home from school. Although Mother sometimes looked through my magazines, I noticed that she never read the stories. It's likely that she even explained to me that the stories weren't appropriate reading for Christians. I don't remember that part. But for some reason I suspected she wouldn't approve of my reading them. So I read the stories secretly.

"I haven't anything else to do, God, except read," I argued. "Surely it's all right for me to read those stories." I couldn't pray that night at all, so I finally just climbed into bed when my sisters did.

The next night, the moment I was on my knees, the whole argument flashed through my mind again. I was still unwilling to yield to the conviction that I shouldn't read such stories.

Again I climbed into bed without saying my prayer.

As the days passed, I grew more and more miserable. I missed talking with God. Doubtless I was an extremely difficult child to live with during that time.

One night, extremely tired, I knelt once more beside my bed.

"Oh, God," I cried, "I'm so miserable. Please forgive me and take away my sin. I won't read any more of those stories if You'll help me not to. Please forgive me for being stubborn and save me that place in heaven. Amen."

The next day was sunny and bright for both me and the weather.

I was sitting on the back steps, gazing at the bright blue sky and the fluffy white clouds, when Mother, passing me as she was bringing water in from the well, asked, "What are you thinking about, Carrol?"

"Why, Mother," I answered, "right behind those clouds is heaven, and God the King is there. He's saving a special place for me because my sins are all forgiven."

I can't help wishing that someone had been able to talk to me more explicitly about God at that time. I was open and willing to know Him then. But I was so young! No one thought of explaining salvation more fully to a child.

I did no better with my own children. As parents we are so busy providing for their physical needs that we often neglect their spiritual nurturing. We expect them to share all their thoughts with us openly. But they seldom do! Perhaps if we adults sought opportunities to discuss in depth the great love of God with our young children, if we told them how Jesus revealed God in human flesh and died for their sins, we might find them sharing their intimate thoughts with us too.

The Bible does tell us that before the creation of the world our salvation was made sure. God *is* saving me that special place right beside Him on His throne. In His perfect timing the Son came into our world and took upon Himself the guilt of our sinful nature, our sinful heredity, our inability to be perfect, our willful transgressions, and died on the cross in our place, to pay the lawful price for our rebellion. Through the death of one man God provided eternal life for all humanity (Rom. 5:15-21). What I needed to understand as a child is that God has given all of this on condition of my active participation in a relationship with Him. And what I need to understand as an adult is that my confidence always rests upon what Jesus did for me on the cross, and I must keep it fresh in my mind. Assurance of my salvation is possible only as I daily maintain an intimate relationship with God.

Now I recognize that God asked me to memorize those special verses in Philippians and Jude to keep fresh in my thoughts the glory, majesty, and praise due to Jesus. It is only as I realize that He was willing to humble Himself to die on the cross, and that God has given Him the name above every name, that I can humble myself to bow before Him in wholehearted worship. Complacency in salvation dies when we realize God's power and majesty.

As we begin to comprehend that Jesus died for our sins, as we view His great love around us, our small faith reaches up and tentatively touches God just as the woman with the hemorrhaging blood touched the hem of Jesus' garment. God floods repentance into our hearts, and we cry out, "I'm a sinner, O Lord; save me! Forgive my willful sinning and change my wayward ways." Repentance is a gift from God, and confession is our response to that gift. God *always* forgives when we honestly confess our sins (Acts 3:19; 5:31; 2 Peter 3:9; 1 John 1:9).

Paul told the jailer at Philippi, "Believe in the Lord Jesus, and you will be saved—you and your household" (Acts 16:31). But we reveal our belief or faith only by our obedience. No one can see our inward faith, but outward obedience is visible to all. We cannot see God the Father, but Jesus came in human flesh to make Him visible. Jesus said, "Why do you call me 'Lord, Lord,' and do not do what I say?" (Luke 6:46). James adds, "Do not merely listen to the word, and so deceive yourselves. Do what it says" (James 1:22).

When we accept Jesus Christ as Lord of our life we become a child of God, and nothing—*nothing*—can separate us from God's love (Rom. 8:35-39). In Jesus we are seated in heavenly places (Eph. 2:6; Col. 3:1-4). Through Him we are right there in that high and lofty place that Isaiah describes.

Jesus uses the delightful little circle of the Godhead to show our inclusion in heaven:

"My prayer is not for them alone. I pray also for those who will believe in me through their message, that all of them may be one, Father, just as you are in me and I am in you. May they also be in us so that the world may believe that you have sent me. I have given them the glory that you gave me, that they may be one as we are one: I in them and you in me. May they be brought to complete unity to let the world know that you sent me and have loved them even as you have loved me" (John 17:20-23).

Who can be saved? "To *all* who received him, to those who believed in his name, he gave the right to become children of God" (John 1:12).

I'm so glad that God often reminds me of how much I mean to Him, how much He loves me, and how easy He has made salvation. (It has to be easy, for I am capable of nothing without Him.) In fact, to most of us salvation sounds too easy. It isn't practical to expect to gain something that great without our paying a great price. We feel sure that there must be something we can do to add to what Christ has done. But Jesus paid the great price. All we can do is submit to Him in worship. And how He delights in our praise, our obedience, our service, our worship! It is through human beings worshiping Him that He plans to light up the whole earth with His glory.

God leaves us free to choose to leave Him if we so desire. Balaam was once a true prophet of God, yet he lost his salvation. King Saul was born again and died a hardened rebel. Satan and his angels were once holy angels dwelling in heaven with God, worshiping Him in spirit and in truth. Each individual makes the choice for salvation or destruction. Unless we consistently practice lifestyle worship, we will one day turn away from God and find ourselves among those in open rebellion against Him. Since God uses no force other than love, we are always left free to choose whom we will worship.

Inspiration calls the destruction of the wicked God's "strange act." But it is a necessary part of God's justice. He will carry it out fully although it breaks His and His Father's heart to do it.

When God described Himself to Moses on the mountain, He told him of His mercy and long-suffering, but then reminded him that He would not leave the guilty unpunished (Ex. 34:6, 7). God knows that in order to have a pure and perfect universe for all eternity He must make a final end of sin. His justice makes it possible for each person to choose His own destiny. But when we have made that choice, justice also requires that we reap its consequences.

A poignant little passage illustrating this appears in Deuteronomy 21. In the last church my husband pastored before his retirement he led us in a study of the book of Deuteronomy for a series of prayer meeting talks. We were blessed as we realized that Moses taught the gospel in the Old Testament. But when we came to this section, it startled me.

"If a man has a stubborn and rebellious son who does not obey his father and mother and will not listen to them when they discipline him, his father and mother shall take hold of him and bring him to the elders at the gate of his town. They shall say to the elders, 'This son of ours is stubborn and rebellious. He will not obey us. He is a profligate and a drunkard.' Then all the men of his town shall stone him to death. You must purge the evil from among you. All Israel will hear of it and be afraid" (verses 18-21).

Since I have three sons of my own, I find it extremely hard to visualize anything that would make me voluntarily give up my sons to death. (Oh, yes, I remember the story of Abraham and Isaac. But God asked Abraham to make a *sacrifice* of his son to a holy God, not take him out to the gate and allow a crowd to stone him because of his rebellion. Isaac was not being punished for any sin on his part. The story of Abraham and Isaac was to be an illustration of God the Father giving His own Son as a sacrifice for us.)

But what purpose could God have for asking the Israelite parents to deliberately offer their sons to be stoned to death? I searched Scripture thoroughly, but could find no story illustrating this practice. The closest possibility I found was God ordering the high priest Aaron not to grieve when fire from the altar killed his two disobedient sons. But it was God Himself who struck them dead in their service to Him. I could understand that story.

I began to wonder if any parent ever really became desperate enough to follow God's advice. But if not, why did the Bible include this little passage? I asked God for more understanding, and slowly I began to see a deeper meaning.

God is a parent, and He has rebellious children with whom He has borne patiently for their entire lifetimes. But the time will come when God will have to say, "These children of mine are stubborn and rebellious. Refusing to obey Me, they are profligates and drunkards. They must be put to death to purge the evil from the universe."

Whether it happened in practice in Israel or not, God used the passage to portray to His people the final destiny of the rebellious. *He* was the parent forced to give up on His rebellious children. How He grieves! But as we worship Him daily, thanking Him for His mercy and His justice, we come to realize that even the terrible destiny of the wicked is part of God's perfect solution to sin. We can be glad that sin and sinners will be no more. Yes, even though some of those who will not share eternal life with us are those we dearly love.

Our worship of God must be built on trust. As our intimacy with Him grows we catch glimpses of God beyond our understanding. But since we find many human things hard to understand, why should we expect to perfectly comprehend the divine? The apostle Paul emphasizes this:

> "Oh, the depth of the riches of the wisdom and
> knowledge of God!
> How unsearchable his judgments,
> and his paths beyond tracing out!
> 'Who has known the mind of the Lord?
> Or who has been his counselor?'
> 'Who has ever given to God, that God should
> repay him?'
> For from him and through him and to him are
> all things.
> To him be the glory forever!
> Amen" (Rom. 11:33-36).

Through Jesus we see the Father and learn to trust Him. Through Him we have learned to recognize the voice of the Holy Spirit as He leads us in a Spirit-filled walk. Because of His supreme sacrifice we are able to confess that Jesus Christ is Lord, to the glory of God the Father.

Summary
True worship must have a foundation as solid as a rock, one not based upon our feelings or our circumstances, for they constantly change. Jesus, the mighty Rock, is the foundation of all true worship.

Jesus came to earth to reveal the Father to us—the high and lofty God, far above the world, omnipotent and omnipresent, surrounded by myriads of angels singing "Holy, Holy, Holy." Because we have never seen the Father, it may be hard for us to make God seem real in our worship.

Worshiping God through Jesus, who was a human being as we are, makes our worship real. God the Father and God the Son share that high and lofty throne. The cross is central to all worship and all praise. Jesus died on the cross for each one of us. Even in praise God wants it to be our personal response to His love. "In order to commune with God, we must have something to say to Him concerning our actual life" (*Steps to Christ*, p. 93).

Before the creation of our world the Godhead planned that God the Son would be the link between heaven and earth. God the Son was the Word that spoke creation into being. In the fullness of God's timing He was born of a virgin and lived a sinless life, but took upon Himself the entire history of human sin and died the death that we deserve. Then God the Father called Him back to heaven, where He is still our representative, interceding daily for us individually, pleading the blood He shed for us as our right to eternal life. The sinless human life that He lived gives us the power for victory over sin and allows us to glorify Him in the world through our witness and our worship.

All of God's gifts come on condition of our active participation in a relationship with Him. God leaves us free to leave Him if we so choose. His justice makes it possible for each person to choose his or her own destiny. But when we have made that choice, that same justice requires that we reap its consequences.

The Lord will finally end sin and sinners. In sorrow He will be forced to put to death some of His dearly loved children. Even the terrible destiny of the wicked is a part of His perfect solution to the sin problem.

Our worship of God must rest solidly on trust. Even though we cannot perfectly understand divine things, through Jesus we can trust God and recognize the voice of the Holy Spirit as He calls us to worship. We will wholeheartedly confess, "Jesus Christ is Lord," and this will be to the glory of God the Father.

CHAPTER 8

Day of Worship

When God created the world He included it in a swirl of time. In the beginning all was darkness, but God immediately created light, and day followed night. The nights and days He marked off into months and years by the movements of the sun and moon and earth.

But even before the months and years added up the accumulation of nights and days, God divided time into seven-day segments that we call weeks. He did this to celebrate the creation of our world. At the close of the sixth day the creation of our world was complete. Animal and plant life filled the earth with sound and beauty. Adam and Eve stood shoulder to shoulder, gazing around them in astonished joy.

"Let's celebrate," God said. "We'll take a day to contemplate what has been accomplished."

Adam and Eve readily agreed although they had little understanding of what the six previous days had meant to God. Perhaps God took that special 24-hour period to tell them all about why and how He had created the world. I can readily imagine that a delegation of angels spent the holy day with God and His newly created human beings in the beauty and peace of the Garden of Eden. The angels must have marveled at the intelligence of the man and woman—and their beauty.

I can imagine that music filled the earth—angelic and human songs of praise—and even God Himself joined in the singing. Surely the angels composed songs about each act of Creation, topping off the music festival with the story of the astounding creation of Adam and Eve. Even the birds and the animals caught the excitement and joy of the celebration of Sabbath.

As the sun set behind the hills and darkness crept over Eden, God told Adam and Eve that it was to be a weekly celebration.

"Every seventh day we'll celebrate anew. You can share with Me your joys and discoveries of the past six days. We'll sing together and delight in each other's company. It will be a holy day."

Adoration on their faces, Adam and Eve agreed. Already their hearts and minds were beginning new songs of praise to their heavenly Father. They could hardly wait for the next seventh day. Worship was the natural response of Adam and Eve to the God who had created them.

God planned that this special 24-hour period of time every seventh day would be holy time, different from the other six days. The special day would be a time to recount Creation, a day for human beings to learn more about God, to worship in music and in testimonial, and to converse face-to-face with God the Son.

Sin, of course, changed the nature of Sabbath worship. No longer was God the Son able to speak with humanity face-to-face. No longer were visible angels able to join humanity in choruses of praise. Yet God knew that, if faithfully observed, the weekly period of holy time would keep communication open between the world and heaven, God's abode.

Throughout Old Testament history those who worshiped God faithfully observed the seventh day as a memorial to Creation. But those who neglected the Sabbath flaunted idol worship before the universe. When God called Abraham from among his idolatrous relatives, it was to give him freedom to worship God in spirit and in truth, and to teach his descendants likewise. Later, when after centuries of slavery in Egypt God again called Abraham's family out of idolatry and slavery to freedom in worship, the first institution He reinstated was the sacredness of the seventh day as a monument to Creation— holy time. As God spoke His commandments in an audible voice from the glory surrounding Mount Sinai, He memorialized Creation in the fourth commandment.

"Remember the Sabbath day by keeping it holy. Six days you shall labor and do all your work, but the seventh day is a Sabbath to the Lord your God. On it you shall not do any work, neither you, nor your son or daughter, nor your manservant or maidservant, nor your animals, nor the alien within your gates. For in six days the Lord made the heavens and the earth, the sea, and all that is in them, but he rested on the seventh day. Therefore the Lord blessed the Sabbath day and made it holy" (Ex. 20:8-11).

The command was not a new revelation to this people. They had grown up with the stories of their heritage ringing in their ears. Thus they should have known about Creation, about the great God who had set aside one seventh of time as special holy time. But as slaves in Egypt they had lost control of their lives— even their time was under Egyptian mandates. Truth had become blurred with idolatry. God knew that His people needed more than freedom from slavery. They needed education, discipline, correction, and clear evidences of His love. All these He patiently gave them throughout 40 years of schooling before He led them into the land He had promised their father, Abraham.

On the borders of the Promised Land Moses, the man whom God had chosen as their deliverer, reminded the Hebrew people of God's marvelous leading throughout their exodus from Egypt and their travels in the desert for the past 40 years. Patiently He recounted God's explicit instructions on how to respond to the covenant He had made with them.

"You were afraid because God spoke with His own voice from the fiery mountain," Moses reminded them, "so I stood between you and God. But God spoke face-to-face with you from out of the fire."

Remembering the glory and majesty of Mount Sinai, the aged leader solemnly repeated the Ten Commandments. When he came to the fourth commandment he incorporated their personal experience of deliverance from slavery as a reason for keeping the seventh day holy.

"Remember that you were slaves in Egypt and that the Lord your God brought you out of there with a mighty hand and an outstretched arm. Therefore the Lord your God has commanded you to observe the Sabbath day" (Deut. 5:15).

As Christians living in the light of the cross we have a third reason for Sabbath observance—redemption. Perhaps it's really the same reason the Hebrews had—once we were slaves to sin, but now we are free in Christ. Although the earth, animals, birds, and plants are important to God, the real reason for their creation was for the enjoyment of humanity. God planned the whole of Creation for us. God's greatest creation was that of a people to be His very own. And the Sabbath will always memorialize that accomplishment.

When Jesus died on the cross just before sundown on Friday, He had finished His earthly work as our substitute, example, and sacrifice. He rested in the grave on the holy hours of the seventh day, making it possible for all humanity once again to rest in the work of God, in which they had no part, and to accept His righteousness and eternal life as a beautiful and precious gift.

In Eden God asked Adam and Eve to celebrate with Him the finished work of Creation week. Adam and Eve had nothing to do with creating the world—they expressed their joy in *God's* accomplishment. Today we have done nothing worthy of celebration. We rest in God's completed work on the cross. Sabbath observance adds nothing to our salvation, but it is a sign of our loyalty and obedience. It is a *gift* God has given us, an opportunity to worship God and commune with Him on holy time.

"Had the Sabbath been universally kept, man's thoughts and

affections would have been led to the Creator as the object of reverence and worship, and there would never have been an idolater, an atheist, or an infidel" (*The Great Controversy*, p. 438).

Ellen White quotes an early Adventist scholar: "'The importance of the Sabbath as the memorial of Creation is that it keeps ever present the true reason why worship is due to God'—because He is the Creator, and we are His creatures. 'The Sabbath therefore lies at the very foundation of divine worship, for it teaches this great truth in the most impressive manner, and no other institution does this. The true ground of divine worship, not of that on the seventh day merely, but of all worship, is found in the distinction between the Creator and His creatures. This great fact can never become obsolete, and must never be forgotten.' (J. N. Andrews, *History of the Sabbath*, chap. 27)" (*ibid.*, pp. 437, 438).

Many Christians today feel that since Jesus clearly ignored the Jewish laws for Sabbathkeeping He negated the fourth commandment. But Jesus Himself said: "Do not think that I have come to abolish the Law or the Prophets; I have not come to abolish them but to fulfil them. I tell you the truth, until heaven and earth disappear, not the smallest letter, not the least stroke of a pen, will by any means disappear from the Law until everything is accomplished" (Matt. 5:17, 18).

By healing on the Sabbath, which was contrary to certain Jewish laws and traditions, Jesus clarified God's original purpose for the Sabbath. Although the Jews strictly observed the Sabbath, some of them had lost the joy of worshiping God during those holy hours because of the burden of seeking to obey all the Sabbath laws added by Jewish teachers and leaders who were trying to ensure that they properly observed the Sabbath. Jesus sought to reveal to them that God had created the Sabbath for humanity's benefit, not as a *means* of salvation, but as an *opportunity* to worship God in a special way. After some accused Him of encouraging His disciples to break the Sabbath, Jesus replied, "The Sabbath was made for man, not man for the Sabbath. So the

Son of Man is Lord even of the Sabbath" (Mark 2:27).

The Son of God had created the Sabbath for our special benefit. It must have grieved Him to see the burden the Sabbath had become to some. He wanted to show humanity how to make the Sabbath the delight it was meant to be. "I created the Sabbath for a blessing for humanity," Jesus was saying. "I am Lord of the Sabbath, so I should know its real purpose."

Ellen White comments about the need we have for this special day of worship and rest:

"God saw that a Sabbath was essential for man, even in Paradise. He needed to lay aside his own interests and pursuits for one day of the seven, that he might more fully contemplate the works of God and meditate upon His power and goodness. He needed a Sabbath to remind him more vividly of God and to awaken gratitude because all that he enjoyed and possessed came from the beneficent hand of the Creator" (*Patriarchs and Prophets*, p. 48).

Had God's true people honored the Sabbath as God planned it, the Bible story would have been greatly different. We need that special holy time to commune with God today. If all Christians spent it in worship and communion with God, we would soon be ready for Jesus' second coming.

Sabbath observance gives each of us another opportunity to worship God in a way that pleases Him. It is ridiculous for a man or woman to seek to worship God while ignoring the plain counsel of Holy Scripture. To do so is to become like Cain, who brought fruits and vegetables to sacrifice to God when He had asked for a lamb!

Jesus gave us His example of church attendance on Sabbath by making a habit of attending services in the synagogue. He knew that legalism and bigotry filled some of the Jewish leaders, yet He showed the value of worshiping in community by attending the services. Among the legalistic crowd at the synagogue were also those who truly worshiped God with warm, loving hearts and kept the Sabbath holy. Jesus identified Himself with them.

Reading Scripture was an integral part of synagogue Sabbath worship. Whenever the words of the Bible are spoken, even by unsanctified lips, the Holy Spirit, through the holy words of God, reaches out to the listener. Jesus desired to be a part of Sabbath worship wherever it was taking place, even if unholy people were present.

He recognized the importance of joining with others in groups to worship God. Jesus knew that we need each other in order to live righteous lives. Perhaps more than at any other time or place, we can grow as we worship God together.

"Then those who feared the Lord talked with each other, and the Lord listened and heard. A scroll of remembrance was written in his presence concerning those who feared the Lord and honored his name.

"'They will be mine,' says the Lord Almighty, 'in the day when I make up my treasured possession. I will spare them just as in compassion a man spares his son who serves him. And you will again see the distinction between the righteous and the wicked, between those who serve God and those who do not'" (Mal. 3:16-18).

Although the prophet Malachi does not specify that the Sabbath is the special time the saints gathered together to talk about God, yet what better time to honor the name of God? The Sabbath is a weekly opportunity to join with others who love the Lord to praise His name.

"Let us hold unswervingly to the hope we profess, for he who promised is faithful. And let us consider how we may spur one another on toward love and good deeds. Let us not give up meeting together, as some are in the habit of doing, but let us encourage one another—and all the more as you see the Day approaching" (Heb. 10:23-25).

The Bible doesn't give us a sample order of service for Sabbath meetings. God left it up to the individual congregations to design services that encourage true worship. Paul describes the early gatherings of followers of Jesus as times when many present took part in the service, some with a hymn, some with a word of instruction, some with a revelation or even speaking in another language, if someone present was able to interpret it so that the message could bless everyone. The varied presentations were all manifestations of the same Holy Spirit. Again the Bible does not specify that these were Sabbath meetings, but Paul does say that such meetings were convened for "the strengthening of the church" and that they should be orderly—"For God is not a God of disorder but of peace" (1 Cor. 14:26-33).

After the synagogues began excluding them, Christians first met in private homes. Eventually some congregations erected church buildings. As Christianity gained political acceptance, Roman political leaders, in a desire for unity and order, encouraged the formalizing and restricting of Christian services to special buildings of worship. There the people were separated from those who were officiating and remained silent unless called upon to speak. Seventh-day worship had already shifted to Sunday worship. People scarcely noted the absence of the Holy Spirit.

I am not against church buildings or orderly services. After all, God designed the wilderness tabernacle and Solomon's Temple, both of which were filled with the Shekinah glory. And one of God's divine attributes is orderliness. Yet I think we need to take care that the exactitude of the form of our services does not hinder the work of the Holy Spirit. God delights in many different styles of worship. Not all cultures or congregations will worship in the same way. What counts, of course, is that we have worshiping hearts. Leadership control should be flexible enough to allow the Spirit to work as He wills. Just changing the style of the way we worship may have little effect upon holiness.

It seems so unimportant to get stirred up over so-called celebration worship. Changing our outward form of worship is only that—a form. And no form has any power or value. God is neither pleased nor displeased by our forms. What does please Him is a humble, contrite, worshiping heart, and what displeases Him is a selfish, proud heart. What we need is to allow God to change our hearts, and then the Spirit will be able to lead us in ways to worship that both please Him and benefit us immensely.

Attending church on the Sabbath is one of its joys. Uniting our voices with others in singing, taking part in reading Scripture, discussing the lesson, praying together, and sharing what God is accomplishing in our lives—all of these draw us closer both to each other and to God. As Christ's return draws nearer, we should be even more careful to assemble on Sabbath to worship. We need each other to spur us on to a more intimate relationship with God and to a larger, more effective witness in the world.

Jesus taught us that the Sabbath was a time especially for healing. This involves not only sickness of the body, but sickness of the soul. The Sabbath is a time for mending relationships both with each other and with God. It allows us to find and give comfort. Sabbath is a wonderful opportunity to invite into our homes those who need healing. Through our friendship and attention the Holy Spirit may be able to melt hard hearts and heal their wounds.

My goal in Sabbathkeeping is not to make up more rules to obey, but to discover more ways to worship God on His holy hours, to make those hours a delight to my children and grandchildren, and to learn more about God.

Because I was born into a Sabbath-observing home, I have a rich heritage of memories of Sabbath worship. I can even remember what Sabbath smelled like when I was a little girl—scrubbed wooden floors, my freshly shampooed hair, and the delightful aroma of some special Sabbath treat—cinnamon rolls, blackberry cobbler, orange tapioca pudding, or something else just as delicious.

The sounds of Sabbath—I can hear them yet! We began the Sabbath just before sundown Friday, with Daddy at the old pump organ, Mother and the three of us girls joining him in singing the old songs: "Love at Home," "There'll Be No Dark Valley When Jesus Comes," "In the Sweet By and By," "Don't Forget the Sabbath," "Jesus Loves Me," "Safely Through Another Week." Then Daddy would read a scripture to us. I can still feel the thrill and challenge of the angel hosts calling to one another while the triumphant Jesus leads a host of redeemed sinners through the gates of the heavenly Jerusalem as Daddy read Psalm 24. (We girls called it "the King of Glory psalm." For years and years it was my favorite. I like it still.)

Sometimes Daddy had us each repeat a Bible verse. Mother says that I was just 2 when I first took part in ushering in the Sabbath with my recitation. Of course, I didn't know any Bible verses, but I knew a Bible story. Mother says they didn't ask me to speak—no one dreamed I'd want to—but when my older sister finished her verse, I spoke up. "Man built house on rock, wind and rain came, and it stay fast. Man built house on sand, wind and rain came, and it fell flat." Even as a 2-year-old I was a real part of the Sabbath worship. The Sabbath was truly made for us, the Johnson girls, and we knew it!

We each prayed to close the sundown service, and then repeated in unison the Lord's Prayer. The next hour or so was the best of all. Although we owned few storybooks, yet Mother found stories appropriate for her small girls in books borrowed from the small church library or from church magazines such as the *Youth's Instructor* or the *Review and Herald,* and she read aloud to us until it was bedtime.

Even bedtime did not end the special feeling we had at our house on the eve of the Sabbath. Daddy often played the old pump organ for an hour or so, and we girls drifted off to dreamland on the wings of sacred song.

Sabbath morning we dressed in our very best and made our way to Sabbath school. Mother usually had a part in the adult program, so we grew up feeling that it was a privilege to help with Sabbath school. Church service, too, was pleasant for us.

Day of Worship

We never read *Our Little Friend,* looked at pictures, or even used a pencil or crayons during the sermon. Instead, we listened or, as children will, merely sat there feeling the happy, loving fellowship of God's big family, the church.

Often company came for Sabbath dinner, but even then no one forgot the children. After dinner Mother read *Our Little Friend* aloud to us all. We would have loved *Primary Treasure* or the *Guide* back in those days! I can still remember some of the stories we heard on those Sabbath afternoons.

If the weather was pleasant, a Sabbath walk was always in order, for both Mother and Daddy loved the outdoors. Daddy would tell us all about how the plants, flowers, and trees grew. We would try to name each bird we saw or heard. Tired, hot, and thirsty, we arrived back home, hurrying to be first in line at the backyard pump for a drink of the cool well water. On rainy Sabbaths we played Bible games and thus gained familiarity with the entire Bible, plus an amazing ability to identify Bible characters.

The closing of the Sabbath was just as pleasant for our family. Again Daddy sat at the organ while we sang. (At one time my ambition was to be able to "sing *big* like Daddy.") Sabbath evening worship was shorter than ushering in the Sabbath the evening before had been. Daddy read another scripture and prayed. As children we were sorry Sabbath was over. Another long week stretched ahead of us before the excitement of the next Sabbath.

I have not a single unpleasant memory of childhood Sabbath observance. Yes, as a teenager I became restless and sometimes felt restricted by the Sabbath. But when I came back home to God at age 19 I settled happily once again into Sabbath worship. I did not keep the Sabbath to earn salvation. My parents, by practice and teaching, taught me righteousness by faith alone. My education in legalism came from elsewhere. For the Johnson family the Sabbath was a day set aside to worship God from love and respect.

Adulthood came all too soon. Seeking to make the Sabbath a delight for three boys and one girl, all within four years and three months of each other in age and in a pastor's family, tried my patience many times. We did not live in the country, where I had grown up. A walk around our neighborhood did not lead to observing nature and worshiping God, but instead to playmates calling my children to join them. I discovered that active young boys are seldom able to sit quietly to listen to stories or play Bible games except for extremely short periods of time. Sabbath was the busiest time of the week for my pastor-husband as he led church activities, but the Sabbath hours dragged for both me and my small children.

With pleasure I observe many young families today as both fathers and mothers plan Sabbath activities for their children. Such children will grow up loving the Sabbath as I did. It will be among their happiest memories. The pastor's family, however, still has a difference. The pastor is father to the entire church and must of necessity and duty see to their congregational needs. Often the Sabbath is his busiest day. A pastor's wife usually needs some extra help to make Sabbath a happy day for her children. Perhaps other families with young children would be willing to include her and her small children along with theirs in some Sabbath activities. Single-parent families have the same need. It's unreasonable to expect that a single person who daily cares for small children will be able to continually provide all that a family needs for happiness. Nearby grandparents or surrogate grandparents from the church membership could be a delightful way to help supply a buoyant "happy Sabbath" in such homes.

Likewise, the necessity today of the mother working outside the home creates a different atmosphere for Sabbath observance. Not only is it difficult for the mother to properly prepare for Sabbath beforehand; one of her greatest needs after a week of outside work is for physical rest. Happy the woman who has a husband ready and willing to go the second mile in making Sabbath a day not only of rest, but of worship, both for mother and children. Happy Sabbathkeeping involves prior planning, especially in homes in which the mother is employed outside the home.

Fortunately my children loved people. As they grew older we filled our house with people on Sabbath—eating together, singing together, laughing and praying. My husband often organized church hikes into the mountains for Sabbath afternoons. Friday nights included group Bible study and guitar singing time. Our children all learned to play musical instruments and spent hours with their music. I felt more successful as a Sabbath mother as the children grew older. The whole church became their family.

With my husband's retirement we find new Sabbath adventures. On the Sabbaths we attend our home church we are able to savor the quietness of time for private devotion and worship even as we sit in the congregation, because we worship without the rush of pastoral responsibility. Sabbath afternoons now also belong to us, not the congregation. We have a whole new realm of Sabbath worship—walks, music, study, rest.

But one of the new Sabbath adventures God has called me to is a ministry of nurturing women's groups and churches. Now it is not as a pastor's wife that I am involved in Sabbath services, but as the speaker! God has ways of opening and closing doors on differing worship patterns.

It's obvious to me that there is no more only one way to worship on Sabbath than there is only one way to pray. But only *one day* is holy time. And if we seek the Lord for guidance, He will lead us to worship on the Sabbath in a way that will fit our family, our church, our age, and our needs.

Sabbathkeeping begins with preparation. The Bible calls Friday the "preparation day." My Friday preparation was the beginning of my Sabbath worship.

The joy of Sabbath is still with me—the smells, the sounds—and I still look forward to Friday. Even now, when we have only my husband, one grown son, and myself in the household, the same weekly ritual takes place. We make every bed in the house up with clean sheets by Thursday bedtime. By sundown Friday the bathrooms are all cleaned, the floors swept or vacuumed, the furniture dusted, the kitchen cleaned, and the refrigerator filled with good food. Friday night dinner is the tastiest of the whole week. Preparing for the Sabbath is still a part of my worship.

Music has always been a vital part of our Sabbath experience. Today, however, it's more often CDs and music videos rather than homemade music. Sometimes, though, my husband makes his own music with his mandolin, or if we have guests, we all join in singing. Quite often we invite friends home from church with us to share the Sabbath noon meal, good fellowship, and maybe a walk down a country lane or around the lake during the afternoon.

I love the Sabbath! What a privilege to share in holy time.

> " 'If you keep your feet from breaking the Sabbath
> and from doing as you please on my holy day,
> if you call the Sabbath a delight
> and the Lord's holy day honorable,
> and if you honor it by not going your own way
> and not doing as you please or speaking idle words,
> then you will find your joy in the Lord,
> and I will cause you to ride on the heights of the land
> and to feast on the inheritance of your father Jacob.'
> The mouth of the Lord has spoken" (Isa. 58:13, 14).

Summary

At Creation God created time for our planet. He divided it into days, weeks, months, and years. The sun governed the day, the moon and stars the night. The movements of the sun, moon, and earth marked off the days and nights into months and years.

But God also divided time into seven-day segments that we call weeks. He did this by taking six days to complete Creation and then adding a special holy day, one He called the Sabbath, asking all humanity to worship Him as Creator of the universe on it. He set the Sabbath apart as holy time.

Even after the entrance of sin into our world, faithful observance of the seventh-day Sabbath kept communication open between earth and heaven. Those who worshiped God observed the Sabbath, while those who rebelled flaunted idol worship before the universe.

When God called out a people to be His very own, the first institution He reinstated was the sacredness of the seventh-day Sabbath as a reminder of Creation. The fourth commandment of the Ten Commandments, written by God's own finger, memorializes the Sabbath for all time.

Although the Jews kept the Sabbath, some loaded it down with so many human-made rules that it became a burden. When Jesus came to earth He sought to restore the joy of the Sabbath to His special people by healing and doing good on the Sabbath. "The Sabbath was made for man," He instructed them, "not man for the Sabbath" (Mark 2:27).

The Sabbath is an opportunity to gather together with fellow Christians to worship God together. Leadership control in a service should be loose enough to allow the Holy Spirit to work upon the congregation, not only as a whole but also individually. Not all congregations will worship in the same way. God's delight is in the worshiping heart, not in the order of service.

We should be even more eager to attend Sabbath services as we come closer and closer to the return of Jesus. All of us need each other to spur us on to a more intimate relationship with Jesus and a more effective witness in the world.

Our goal today in Sabbathkeeping should be to discover exciting new ways to worship God on His holy hours, to make the Sabbath a delight for our children, neighbors, and friends, and to learn more about Him.

Sabbath observance begins with preparation. We should ready our homes and our hearts to worship God in a special way on His holy day.

CHAPTER 9

Last Great Call to Worship

One of the most exciting things I encountered when I began sanctuary prayer was new insights to God's plan for worship during the final pre-Advent judgment. Raised in a Seventh-day Adventist home, attending church school from elementary through college, I had a good foundation in Adventist doctrines. I knew well our belief in the investigative judgment of the righteous just before Jesus returns to earth to reward His saints with eternal life. But it didn't mean that I understood all I knew—or that I was at peace with it.

I remember listening to my husband preach sermons on the two covenants, the time prophecies of Daniel, and the investigative judgment, and marveling at his ability to put together sermons on the topics. (Actually, what I would do on those Sabbath mornings was just put my exhausted mind on "hold" and think my own thoughts. I was so good at daydreaming!)

I'll just never understand all this, I thought. *Why does Christianity have to be so complicated? Why can't Bible teaching relate to daily life?*

I never imagined that the time would come when those very topics would relate to my life so completely that they would be what held my life together. Or that I myself would one day preach sermons centered on the subjects!

God introduced judgment time to the world with a call to worship. "Then I saw another angel flying in midair, and he had the eternal gospel to proclaim to those who live on the earth—to every nation, tribe, language and people. He said in a loud voice, 'Fear God and give him glory, because the hour of his judgment has come. Worship him who made the heavens, the earth, the sea and the springs of water'" (Rev. 14:6, 7).

The angel summons all the earth to worship. Whom are they to worship? The God who created the heavens, the earth, and the sea. By employing the very words used to describe God in the fourth commandment, in which He reminded His people of the sacredness of the seventh day, God links this message with the Sabbath day of rest.

How are they to worship? Two more angels follow the first with astonishing messages of approaching doom for the world's inhabitants. A choice in worship determines their fate. Those who worship the beast will drink from the cup of God's wrath. "There is no rest day or night for those who worship the beast and his image, or for anyone who receives the mark of his name" (Rev. 14:11).

But both passages also end with counsel for those who heed the first angel's call to worship God. "This calls for patient endurance on the part of the saints who *obey God's commandments and remain faithful to Jesus*" (Rev. 14:12).

It will take patience and endurance to worship God when all the world is following the beast! Obviously worshiping God includes obedience to His commandments and faith in Jesus.

When I began employing the steps the sanctuary reveals for personal prayer, God was able to begin the process of showing me how every Bible teaching relates to daily life. He took my one-sided understanding of the pre-Advent judgment and showed me His great last call to the world to worship Him.

More people today than ever before in earth's history are awakening to a recognition of judgment—most in fear, I must admit—but some in expectation, as did the Jews. The Jews of Christ's time eagerly awaited the judgment, believing that God would then vindicate them before all their enemies. But they would not accept Christ's teaching about what the judgment meant.

All Christians recognize the necessity of judgment in order to separate the saved from the unsaved. But few think deeply enough to realize that it must occur before Christ comes to reward His saints. If the judgment has not already taken place, how will He know whom to reward? The confusion, of course, is because the Bible speaks of three phases of judgment: the judgment of the righteous, which must be done before Jesus comes; the judgment of the wicked, completed during the 1,000 years; and the executive stage of judgment, in which the wicked receive their punishment at the end of the millennium.

Today God is preparing a people whom He can translate to heaven without seeing death. They must reach Christian maturity (being able to recognize truth from error), they must understand God's character of love and justice, and they must be obedient to all of God's commandments. Christians who have died in the past, not understanding some of the truths important to the last days, God can safely save because they loved Him with their whole hearts and were obedient in all they understood. But God must now have a people who will light up the whole world with His glory. The earth must be filled with the knowledge of God.

How can Christians sincerely worship God in spirit and in truth unless they understand His character of love and justice? But how can they understand it if spiritual things seem to have no practical application to their daily life?

The sanctuary led me to the specific time and place that God has set aside for worshiping Him with heart-searching and intensity. The ancient priests entered the Most Holy Place only one day a year in the sanctuary services. The Day of Atonement, the tenth day of the seventh month of the Jewish calendar, was the most solemn day of the year for the Israelites. On that day each Hebrew refrained from work and afflicted his or her soul, searching the heart for buried sin to confess before the Lord.

Of course, being Adventist educated, I knew t'
of Atonement prefigured the pre-Advent work of judgment ..
Jesus, our high priest, is doing right now in heaven. But heaven
is far away, and I had no way of seeing what is going on there,
so it all seemed extremely secretive and mysterious.

In school my teachers had taught me that Daniel's time
prophecies pointed to 1844 as the beginning of the time prefigured by the Day of Atonement. It was the period when the
first angel began shouting his message. At that time Jesus, as
our high priest, began a new phase of His high-priestly work:
the pre-Advent judgment. He began going through the books
of heaven to decide who was to be saved and who was to be
lost. Jesus would consider the record of every person whose
name had ever been entered in the book of life, beginning with
Adam and Eve and all who have claimed God the Son as their
Redeemer down through the ages, and then progressing to
those who are still alive. If He found any unconfessed sin on the
record, He stamped the page with a large red "LOST." (I'm not
at all sure my teachers specified that the stamp was red! My
vivid imagination likely supplied the color.)

My response as a young student was not one of confidence.
How did I know if I had confessed every sin written against me?
I had only one comfort as a young person. I figured it might
take Jesus quite a while to complete His search of the records
of the dead. Maybe I would have time to become perfect before
He got to my name. In the meanwhile I tried to put out of my
mind the prospect of His reaching my name and checking my
record. I sought to live a good Christian life, every day confessing my known sins. Thoughts of the large red "LOST"
stamp led only into nightmares.

Since this is not a book about prophecy, I will not go into
time prophecies, but only state that I believe wholly in the va-
lidity and truth of the Seventh-day Adventist interpretation of
the pre-Advent judgment. However, my teachers stopped short
of applying it in any practical way to my life experience. I sus-

pect they did so because they understood no better than I did! They taught me only what they knew.

As I grew older I began to recognize a serious gap in my understanding. It was obvious to me that Jesus must by now be nearing the time when He would begin working on the records of the living. And how was He conducting His search, anyway? Was He going by chronological order, alphabetical order, by families, localities—or what? With the advent of computers I also began to consider that it was rather ridiculous to picture Jesus toiling away at His books for years and years when even here on earth, with computers, we could almost immediately accomplish tasks that once took months and years. Surely heaven has better and faster equipment for recordkeeping than earth has! Then, too, it was obvious that in spite of my dedication and prayers sin still festered in my life.

One day I was further disheartened to discover a passage in which Ellen White instructed us to tell our neighbors the good news about the judgment.

"Lord, how can I tell anyone something I don't understand?" I complained to God. "I really don't think my neighbors would consider it good news that You are taking such a long time getting through Your bookkeeping! I don't see anything that sounds to me like good news in the judgment."

When God showed me that He had set up the sanctuary in the wilderness to reveal how He saves each human soul, and I began praying step-by-step through the sanctuary, I started questioning God in earnest.

"Why do You keep the work of judgment such a secret?" was one of my first questions when I came to the Most Holy Place in sanctuary prayer. "I have no idea what You have written about me in Your book. I don't even know what sins You have recorded against me. I have confessed what I know to be sin, but more and more I realize I don't even know myself! How can I possibly have a clean record through confession and Your forgiveness when there is no doubt that I don't even confess the right sins?"

In desperation one day I burst out, "Why can't You just send me a computer printout of my page in Your book so that I can know the sins recorded there? Why is it all so *secret?*"

Patiently God answered. He has no desire to keep any of it secret. In fact, His purpose throughout the day of atonement is to reveal, not conceal. Before He completes the work of judgment and the cleansing of the heavenly sanctuary, and every case closes, God in mercy speaks to every honest-hearted Christian who has learned to hear His voice, revealing to them any unconfessed sin still upon their record page—not just sins of the past or of commission, but sins of thought, motive, the way we treat people, the way we live our daily lives, the sins that we commit every day. God must have a pure people who are so wholehearted for Him that they can reveal His character to the world. Ellen White explains it like this:

"The great plan of redemption, as revealed in the closing work for these last days, should receive close examination. The scenes connected with the sanctuary above should make such an impression upon the minds and hearts of all that they may be able to impress others. All need to become more intelligent in regard to the work of the atonement, which is going on in the sanctuary above. When this grand truth is seen and understood, those who hold it will work in harmony with Christ to prepare a people to stand in the great day of God, and their efforts will be successful. By study, contemplation, and prayer God's people will be . . . brought into harmony with Christ and His great work of cleansing the sanctuary above from the sins of the people. Their faith will go with Him into the sanctuary, and the worshipers on earth will be carefully reviewing their lives and comparing their characters with the great standard of righteousness. They will see their own defects; they will also see that they must have the aid of the Spirit of God if they would become qualified for the great and solemn work for this time which is laid upon God's ambassadors" (*Testimonies,* vol. 5, p. 575).

This special time of judgment, the work Jesus is doing as

our high priest in the Most Holy Place in heaven, is vital to end-ing sin in the world. God plans that those who will be alive when He comes to earth again will spend this time as the Israelites did during the Day of Atonement—in heart-searching and prayer. He wants to reveal to us our inmost desires, the sins hidden even from ourselves. Without our cooperation Christ is unable to do this.

When we confess and repent of the sins God reveals to us in His judgment work, He will be able to close the books, end probationary time for mortals, and take His children home. After that will come the entire conclusion of sin, when He lets the wicked reap the results of their choices.

Because I have such a need for my Christianity to be prac-tical, God opened up to me a simple outline of what the pre-Advent judgment means in the life of a Christian today. When we begin to catch a glimpse of God's activity in our behalf, our faith will grow! And with growing faith we can cooperate with Him more fully in His judgment work. What is taking so long is not Jesus' inability to sift through His paperwork, but the lack of cooperation on the part of His people. God is not will-ing that *any* of His children perish. When we understand and cooperate with Him, the work will quickly finish.

Judgment and worship have a vital connection. God is looking for a people who will worship Him in *spirit,* from the very depths of their heart, and in *truth,* understanding the char-acter of God and what He is doing in their lives personally and what He is doing in heaven to conclude the reign of sin. God is nauseated with halfheartedness, double-mindedness, and luke-warmness. Ignorance and error grieve Him.

The Pre-Advent Judgment

We can divide God's work of judgment into three distinct parts, each an aspect of His efforts on our behalf: *investigation, discipline,* and *instruction.* The three parts intertwine and mingle in our life experience, but understanding each of them separately helps us to accept and cooperate with what God is doing in our lives.

Investigation

This first phase has three parts:

1. *God examines my actions, thoughts, and motives.* Again and again throughout Scripture God reiterates the fact that He, Creator and God, searches the human heart and mind, intimating that what God finds in the heart of each of us will determine His final judgment in our behalf. "I the Lord search the heart and examine the mind, to reward a man according to his conduct, according to what his deeds deserve" (Jer. 17:10). "For a man's ways are in full view of the Lord, and he examines all his paths" (Prov. 5:21).

2. *God asks us to examine our own hearts.* "Examine yourselves to see whether you are in the faith; test yourselves. Do you not realize that Christ Jesus is in you—unless, of course, you fail the test?" (2 Cor. 13:5).

The danger in the second part of investigation is that I don't always agree with God's evaluation. I don't see myself as God views me, or even as others regard me. A teacher of mine once said that each of us is three people—the person we think we are, the person others see, and the person God knows that we actually are.

While it is important that I examine myself, I must remember that God's knowledge of me is always true, while my appraisal of myself will most likely be faulty. Therefore, I must always test my own search by the Word of God. When I can accept God's conclusions as wholly true I can repent and receive forgiveness and cleansing. God is in the work of "at-one-ment," making us at one with Him in our desire for righteousness. The results of my heart search must become identical with God's judgment in order for me to feel the need for repentance. I must say "Yes!" to God. God must have my complete cooperation before He can complete His loving work of judgment for me and in me.

One word of caution as we go about the work of examining ourselves:

"'Examine yourselves, whether ye be in the faith.'" Some conscientious souls, on reading this, immediately begin to criticize their every feeling and emotion. But this is not correct self-examination. It is not the petty feelings and emotions that are to be examined. The life, the character, is to be measured by the only standard of character, God's holy law. The fruit testifies to the character of the tree. Our works, not our feelings, bear witness of us.

"The feelings, whether encouraging or discouraging, should not be made the test of the spiritual condition. By God's Word we are to determine our true standing before Him" (*Review and Herald*, Feb. 28, 1907).

The greatest share of my work of investigation is learning to agree with God's evaluation.

3. *The intelligent creatures in the universe investigate and observe us.* This third section of investigation comprises part of the larger picture of God's plan, not only for our world, but for the universe. Commenting on 1 Corinthians 4:9, Ellen White says:

"The inhabitants of unfallen worlds and of the heavenly universe are watching with intense interest the conflict between good and evil. They rejoice as Satan's subtleties, one after another, are discerned and met with 'It is written,' as Christ met them in His conflict with the wily foe. Every victory gained is a gem in the crown of life. In the day of victory all the universe of heaven triumphs. The harps of the angels send forth the most precious music, accompanying the melody of the voice" (letter 5, 1900, in *The SDA Bible Commentary,* Ellen G. White Comments, vol. 7, p. 1088).

The angels and the inhabitants of unfallen worlds and Satan and his angels view—and yes, even examine—my life! Of course, only God is my judge. But if God is to have a perfectly happy and sinless universe throughout eternity, peopled with intelligent creatures, then He must answer all the questions concerning His character now, before our world ends and God creates a new one.

The angels and the beings on the unfallen worlds eagerly watch to see if God's plan really transforms my life. By now, of course, they have seen it work notably in the lives of such people as Enoch, Noah, Abraham, Moses, David, Paul, and unnamed others—although pitifully few in comparison with the total number of the world's inhabitants. God Himself became a man. As Jesus He gave a perfect example of how the plan can change sinful humanity.

It is important that God be able to defend Himself to the rest of the universe when He gives me eternal life. It must be apparent that I have accepted Jesus' sacrifice for my sins, received a new heart, been endowed with the power of the Holy Spirit, and am living His life of obedience. Citizens of the universe must be sure that I will not threaten eternity. It is vital to their future happiness.

God's honor rests upon my life. It is an awesome thought to realize that when I sin I place God in a bad light before His universe. "[God's] intent was that now, through the church, the manifold wisdom of God should be made known to the rulers and authorities in the heavenly realms, according to his eternal purpose which he accomplished in Christ Jesus our Lord" (Eph. 3:10, 11).

Everyone who professes the name of Christian is on display before the universe. I dislike the thought that the universe includes the devil, but it surely does. Whenever I fall into sin, he or his demons taunt Jesus and the holy angels.

"Look at Carrol," they exult. "Isn't she supposed to be one of Your saints? She's no better than our followers. Worse than some of them. The plan of redemption simply does not work. It is impossible to obey God's laws. She is evidence of it."

But two things always silence God's critics. First, Jesus lived a perfect sinless life despite the accumulated effects of sin. The plan worked. Second, I have confessed my sin and repented, and am relying entirely upon Jesus for my salvation. The plan works still.

Discipline

The second way that God works in judgment is through discipline, which has two parts.

1. *Cutting.* We're all familiar with the cutting part of discipline—trials, persecution, and suffering. They are the tools God uses in disciplining us. And we don't like them!

"My son, do not despise the Lord's discipline and do not resent his rebuke, because the Lord disciplines those he loves, as a father the son he delights in" (Prov. 3:11, 12).

The writer of Hebrews quotes the same two verses from Proverbs in Hebrews 12 and then goes on to comment:

"Endure hardship as discipline; God is treating you as sons. For what son is not disciplined by his father? If you are not disciplined (and everyone undergoes discipline), then you are illegitimate children and not true sons. Moreover, we have all had human fathers who disciplined us and we respected them for it. How much more should we submit to the Father of our spirits and live! Our fathers disciplined us for a little while as they thought best; but God disciplines us for our good, that we may share in his holiness. No discipline seems pleasant at the time, but painful. Later on, however, it produces a harvest of righteousness and peace for those who have been trained by it" (Heb. 12:7-11).

James speaks of trials in such glowing terms that it almost makes me covet them! "Consider it pure joy, my brothers, whenever you face trials of many kinds, because you know that the testing of your faith develops perseverance. Perseverance must finish its work so that you may be mature and complete, not lacking anything" (James 1:2-4).

But when I am in the midst of a trial I have difficulty finding anything joyous about it! Yet one day in the midst of grieving I discovered the second part of discipline, and it turned my sorrow into joy!

2. *Healing.* I found that God has an antidote for every sorrow: His wonderful healing of comfort, peace, and joy.

I was standing at the kitchen sink, contemplating the cutting God was doing in my life. One sorrow just seemed to swell and roll into another sorrow. There seemed no end to grief.

"I can't bear any more, Father," I cried. "Surely this is enough. I cannot stand to grieve any longer."

God answered me immediately.

"Why are you complaining, Carrol, when I consider you worthy to share in My suffering?"

I paused in my dishwashing, hardly daring to believe I had heard God aright. Me, worthy to share in His suffering?

"Oh, Father," I breathed, "this is Your suffering?" I gulped down the sorrow that clogged my throat and tried a smile. Could it be true that this was really God's suffering? I had always thought that in order to share in the suffering of Christ I would have to be put in prison for my faith in God or be persecuted by my neighbors because I kept the Sabbath. My present sorrow was a family matter, seemingly unrelated to God. Yet God immediately assured me that He allowed no suffering to come to me that did not first of all afflict Him.

The comfort of the thought brightened my life for many a day. How few, even of Christians, realize the availability of God's healing comfort as a balm for the necessary cutting. If we only realized how near God is in our trials, how soon we could find the comfort of His healing!

Both Hosea and Isaiah speak of the cutting and the healing. "Come, let us return to the Lord. He has torn us to pieces but he will heal us; he has injured us but he will bind up our wounds" (Hosea 6:1). "The Lord binds up the bruises of his people and heals the wounds he inflicted" (Isa. 30:26).

Ellen White says, "All trials that are received as educators will produce joy" (*Lift Him Up*, p. 249).

Instruction

The third part of judgment is instruction. God intends to fill the whole world with knowledge of Him. He wants especially to teach us in four special areas.

1. *God wants to teach us about Himself.* The increased understanding of righteousness by faith spreading over Christianity is part of God's special plan for us to understand His character of love. Of course, in order for this to have any real meaning in our lives individually, we must study it for ourselves and *experience* the intimacy with God it leads to.

2. *God wants to teach us how to understand ourselves,* why we act the way we do. Modern medical science is providing us new understanding of the brain and how it works, and the importance of the memories. God desires that we be able to reach out to Him from the innermost core of our mind, releasing buried resentment, anger, and hurt. Then we can worship Him with our whole hearts, undivided by selfishness, confused thinking, and false teaching.

And in understanding and accepting ourselves honestly, as God views us, we can reach out and accept others with God's unconditional love.

3. *He wants to teach us more truth about Bible doctrines and prophecy than any former generation has ever understood.* We never honor God through ignorance or error. Nor can He any longer overlook it. Understanding is crucial to cooperation with God in His judgment work. If we earnestly seek Him, God will lead us into all truth.

4. *God wants to make us thorough and honest workers.* Being willing learners in all three of the above areas will lead us to become faithful in everything we do. Just as God gifted human beings as able workers to build the sanctuary in the wilderness, He will instruct us in our practical work. Shoddy workmanship never glorifies God. He wants to make us thorough and honest carpenters, secretaries, teachers, doctors, nurses, businesspeople, salespeople, mothers, and fathers.

Last Great Call to Worship

About six years ago, in a city not far from where I live, a church congregation built a beautiful new church. They delighted in its beauty. But a few months ago the county inspectors condemned the buildings as unsafe to use anymore. It was a shock to that congregation! Their lovely new church was dangerous because the builders did not faithfully follow the specifications of the architectural plans and used inferior materials. Careless Christian workers publicly dishonored God in that city.

God's plan for His last generation is that they will light up the whole world with their reflection of the character of God—by their love of God and their love for each other (and even sinners), by their clear understanding and explanations of Bible doctrine and prophecy, and by their transparent honesty and carefulness in all earthly matters.

In the pre-Advent judgment God is carefully selecting a people who walk with Him in intimacy. He will be able to reveal to them His most important thoughts. Even amid the traumatic events of the close of earth's history His people will find joy in the presence of Jesus. They will worship God in spirit and in truth. The judgment is *good news!*

Summary

The central theme of the pre-Advent judgment is worship. God must have a group of followers who worship Him in Spirit and in truth to light up the whole world with His glory before He can come again with the reward of everlasting life in His hands to give to those waiting for Him.

All Christians recognize the necessity of some sort of judgment to separate the saved from the unsaved. But few think deeply enough to realize that God must do it before Christ comes to reward His saints. They often mix up the prophecies of the judgment of the righteous (which must happen before Christ comes) with prophecies about the judgment of the wicked (accomplished during the 1,000 years) and with prophecies concerning the pronouncement of punishment given at the close of the 1,000 years, when sin finally comes to an end.

God can safely save those Christians who died in the past and were obedient in all that they understood about God even though they did not grasp all the truths being revealed to Christians in these last days. But those Christians who are alive when Jesus comes must worship Him fully, understanding truth as revealed in the Word of God, and be obedient to God's commandments.

The sanctuary leads us to the specific time and place that God has set aside for worshiping Him in heart-searching and intensity. The priest entered the Most Holy Place only one day a year. On that day each Hebrew was to refrain from work and afflict his soul, searching his heart for buried sin to confess before the Lord. The Day of Atonement prefigured the work that Christ would do in the Most Holy Place in heaven during the pre-Advent judgment beginning in 1844. (For a clear understanding of the prophecies of Daniel 7, which point to the fall of 1844 as the beginning of the prophetic day of atonement, read Clifford Goldstein's *1844 Made Simple* [Pacific Press, 1988].)

Here is an outline of how the pre-Advent judgment relates to the daily life of a Christian:

Three Parts to the Pre-Advent Judgment

I. *Investigation.* Investigation has three parts:

1. *God examines my actions, thoughts, and motives.* His examination always reveals truth.

2. *God asks us to search our own hearts.* The greatest share of my investigation is learning to agree with God's evaluation.

3. *The intelligent creatures of the universe investigate and observe us.* If God is to have a perfectly happy and sinless universe throughout eternity, then He must answer all questions about His character now. And the angels and other unfallen beings must be sure that we will not create a disturbance in eternity. All our desire for sin must be eliminated.

II. *Discipline.* Discipline has two parts:

1. *Cutting.* Trials, persecution, and suffering are necessary to prepare us for eternity.

2. *Healing.* Comfort, peace, and joy are available immediately as an antidote to every sorrow.

III. Instruction. Instruction has four parts:

1. *God wants to teach us about Himself.* In order to worship God fully, we need to understand His character of love.

2. *God wants to teach us how to understand ourselves,* what makes us act and think as we do. He longs for us to be able to reach out to Him from the very innermost core of our minds, releasing buried resentment, anger, and hurt. Then we can accept others unconditionally and worship God with our whole hearts.

3. *He wants to teach us more truth about Bible doctrines and prophecies than any former generation has ever understood.* Our ignorance and error do not glorify Him. Understanding is crucial to His judgment work.

4. *He wants to make us thorough and honest workers* so that we can glorify God in whatever we do. The same God who gave gifts of workmanship to aid in building the sanctuary in the wilderness will teach each of us to be skillful in everything that we must do.

God's plan for His last generation is that they will light up the whole world with their reflection of the character of God—by their love of God and their love for each other (and even sinners), by their clear understanding and explanations of Bible doctrine and prophecy, and by their transparent honesty and carefulness in all earthly matters.

CHAPTER 10

How to Implement Worship in Your Own Life

Very few changes in human behavior ever happen except by deliberate choice. It's true that the apple tree bears apples because it is an apple tree. But then the tree has no mind or will of its own. The tree metaphor goes only so far. God made Adam and Eve intelligent beings who could choose to do otherwise than He had made them to do. He created them only for good works. But they chose bad works.

As Christians we'd like to think that our initial encounter with God in the new birth has so changed us that we can yield to our feelings and automatically live righteous lives. Life would be so easy that way, just doing what we want to do. But we are not trees. God has chosen to create for Himself a people who through moment-by-moment cooperation with Him against the constant pull of the flesh, the world, and the devil develop righteous characters that will stand forever.

His purpose is to re-create human beings into creatures who are so Godlike in thought and action that the entire Godhead—the Father, the Son, and the Holy Spirit—can enjoy conversing with them throughout eternity. Think of it—carrying on a spirited conversation with God that challenges and delights Him with the keenness of our reasoning and understanding! Impossible? I think not. His plans contain far more than we can even dream of, for who can understand the mind of God?

Although He built in us the desire to worship, the direction of worship is ever our choice, and we can multiply our enjoyment of an intimate relationship with God through deliberately putting moments of worship into our lives.

The sanctuary illustration reveals special times that are appropriate for worship. The morning and evening sacrifices prefigured the God-fearing household gathering together for morning and evening worship. Individually we find specific blessings in personal worship at the beginning and the close of each day. Then again we discover prefigured special Sabbath worship in the Sabbath ritual of the priest eating the bread from the table of God's presence. To me this suggests the pastor sharing the bread of life with his congregation.

Of course, no time is inappropriate for worship. We have no idea what day or what time of day God halted Moses at the burning bush to worship, or when He gave Isaiah his vision of heaven, or when He interrupted Saul on the way to Damascus.

But the sanctuary leads us to one more specific time that God has set aside for worshiping Him with heart-searching and intensity. The Day of Atonement that we talked about in the previous chapter was the most solemn day of the year for the Israelites. On that day each Hebrew was to refrain from work and search his or her heart for hidden motives or forgotten sin to confess before the Lord. It prefigured the pre-Advent work of judgment being done in heaven right now by Jesus, our high priest. Since the real day of atonement is not a single 24-hour day, but a period of time that extends from 1844 until Jesus completes His judgment of the living, we of course have to carry on our necessary business in order to live. But the center of our focus should always be Jesus, His sacrifice on the cross, and His role as high priest that concludes the work of salvation prefigured by the sanctuary illustration.

We live in a specific time God set apart for us to worship Him in spirit and in truth. Our generation, more than any generation before us, should faithfully spend time in worship.

God loves to call us to special times of worship. We often miss them because of our preoccupation with earthly affairs, lack of contemplation, and misunderstanding. As our relationship with God develops into greater intimacy, more and more we will hear His call and respond.

In this closing chapter I want to share with you some ideas of how you can enrich your relationship with God by deliberately adding special moments of worship. Because I am excited about what God is doing in my life through following the sanctuary illustration for my personal prayers, I may sound as if I am telling you that you have to pray, praise, and worship just as I do. But I don't really think that! My ways will not be suitable for all of you. What I desire is that each of you will reach out toward God in the manner that He impresses you to pray, praise, and worship. No exercise, either for worship, praise, or prayer, has any meaning other than to make real in your experience a relationship with God, a growing intimacy with a God worthy of worship.

Of course, the time for worship to begin each day is as you awaken. Our first thoughts should be of God and His marvelous gift of life, both now and for eternity. Then as you go into your morning devotional time your heart will be tuned in to hear God's voice. But my special emphasis in this chapter is on other deliberate times set aside for worship throughout the day. You may need to sandwich such moments during lunchtime at your place of employment, in the car as you drive to work or home again, on Sabbaths or Sundays, or on vacationtime. If you are retired or a homemaker, or if you work at a home-based business, you may be able to accommodate worshiptimes more freely.

Music, praise, and Scripture are the voice of worship. When I worked as a school librarian for 15 years I often worshiped in the car going to work by singing, meditation, and praying aloud. My favorite song during those days was a chorus of commitment, "I Have Decided to Follow Jesus." Another old-fashioned favorite was "I'm a Child of the King."

Not long ago I needed to spend several hours working in my sewing room, preparing dolls to sell in my shop in an antique mall. But I also felt a keen desire to worship. So I picked out several CDs of worship music (I chose three by Ponder, Jennings, and Harp; one by the Heralds Quartet; plus "Joyful, Joyful," by the Wedgwood Trio with Del Delker) and played them all morning. It's very easy to let music fade into the background as you work unless you specifically sharpen your listening powers and deliberately worship along with the music. Sometimes as a CD ended and before I put in a new one I would praise God vocally. And sometimes I would sing along and lift my hands in praise and worship. (When you're alone in a room with God you can express yourself freely in worship, with no thought of what any spectators might say!)

When I left the sewing room to cook dinner for my husband and son, I carried with me a spirit of worship and refreshment. I intend to do this more often.

Since music is an integral part of worship, anything that incorporates worship music into your home can be a time of worship. Sing along with tapes and CDs. Deliberately memorize the words to worship music, either choruses or hymns, and especially praise music that uses words of Scripture. Or sit down with your hymnal and choose a song you especially enjoy and memorize all the stanzas.

A dear friend and prayer partner, Virginia Collins, told me that she sometimes worships by choosing a song for each step of sanctuary prayer—singing through the sanctuary! I can hardly wait to try it. She begins with a praise song, often the first song in *The Seventh-day Adventist Hymnal*, "Praise to the Lord." She goes on to "All to Jesus I Surrender," "Whiter Than Snow," and other appropriate hymns. (If you'd like to try this and have never practiced sanctuary prayer, turn back to chapter 2 of this book, which lists seven steps the sanctuary shows us for personal prayer, and choose a hymn or chorus for each of the seven steps.) Virginia has a great stock of hymns ready on the tip of her tongue to sing, for she habitually takes her hymnal along in the car as she drives to her many appointments, memorizing the words to the songs as she drives. (Her husband, Ed, often worries about this! How can she drive and look at the hymnal at the same time? Virginia assures him that she is very careful and glances at the book only at stoplights, or just a quick peek to verify a word. Somehow, even though Virginia has never had an accident, Ed still doesn't seem convinced that singing from a hymnal while driving a car is a safe practice!)

Another way I occasionally like to worship is by setting aside a 24-hour period to fast and pray. I'm not very good at fasting, for I seem to have borderline low blood sugar. But I have found that by drinking lots of water and fruit juices I can comfortably fast for a 24-hour period if I begin my fast right after the main meal of the day (for our family that is usually between 2:00 and 3:00 P.M.) and end it with a light meal 24 hours later. I have been attracted to fasting as a part of worship ever since I read Andrew Murray's *With Christ in the School of Prayer* (New York: Grosset and Dunlap). Murray says that the significance of fasting is taking hold of heaven through prayer and letting go of the earth through fasting. "Prayer is the one hand with which we grasp the invisible; fasting, the other with which we let loose and cast away the visible" (p. 88).

Especially while writing a manuscript I will sometimes fast in special worship. I want my books to be the result of grasping the invisible.

A friend suggested another way to fast. She calls it the "Daniel" fast. Instead of abstinence from all food, she limits herself to very plain food, such as fruits and vegetables with no oils or sweets. It can remind us that Jesus fasted in the wilderness for 40 days, winning victory for every believing soul over any passion or appetite (*appetite* meant primarily "passion" and "drive" during Mrs. White's time) that threatens to control us. Jesus will strengthen us to deny ourselves for His glory.

A third fast does not involve food. When I was an academy librarian I often totally abstained from all TV or secular reading for the week just before the school Week of Prayer, devoting my mind entirely to prayer for the students. Often during that week a group of students met with me during the lunch hour to pray for one another and the student body as a whole, that the Week of Prayer would draw students and faculty closer to the Lord.

No kind of fasting earns any points with God. What fasting does is make real in our experience what we profess to believe. It shows that we are serious about our commitment to God and a life of holiness.

God talks in Isaiah 58 about the difference between fasting as an expression of our devotion to God and fasting as a meaningless ritual. He rebuked the Israelites for fasting as a way of seeming to be eager to listen to Him yet paying no attention to what He had to say to them. What good is a fast, God asked, when you just go on doing as you please?

Then God listed the kind of fast He would really value: to loose the chains of injustice, set the oppressed free, give food to the hungry, provide shelter for the homeless, clothe the naked, care for our families, and stop accusing and speaking maliciously of others (Isa. 58:6-10).

Any fast we choose to aid us in worship must always be honest and remember God's identification of fasting with lifestyle worship. We should not fast to receive approval from God, but rather to accompany our heartfelt submission.

Ellen White suggests spending an hour each day contemplating the life of Christ, especially its closing scenes. A good worship exercise, it praises the Father, the Son, and the Holy Spirit for the great plan of redemption.

Another way I like to worship is by reading stories of special worship encounters by Bible characters, noting how God met them and their response. Moses is perhaps my favorite because I so identify with him in his late call to the ministry. Like him, I feel inadequate to be a spokesperson for God, yet thankful for the opportunities. I want to worship as wholeheartedly as Moses did. Other favorites are Isaiah; Jeremiah; Ezekiel; Hannah; the child Samuel; David; Mary, the mother of Jesus; Elizabeth, the mother of John the Baptist; the apostle Paul; John the revelator; and Peter. Perhaps you can discover others to study in your worshiptime.

When my pastor-husband retired, we built a home on a mountain lot we had owned for more than 30 years. Often during that 30 years we would drive up the winding mountain roads and look our lot over with yearning in our hearts. The great pines and cedars and oaks became friends. But it seemed unreal that we would ever live in that quiet mountain atmosphere. City communities were more familiar. But our day came. Now we call squirrels, raccoons, chipmunks, coyotes, bears, wildcats, opossums, and numerous birds our neighbors. It is a joy to sometimes join nature in worshiping God outdoors! When I hear a western tanager sing I wonder if the angels really sing more beautifully. The dozens of little house wrens that nest in our big pine tree and in the surrounding bushes and trees make springtime alive with music as lovely as any choir I have ever heard. The flashing blue of jays and bluebirds in swift flight, the brilliant yellow of that elusive tanager who sings in the tops of the trees, and the orange elegance of the pair of orioles that often dart up onto our deck to sneak a drink from the hummingbird feeder are foretastes of Eden made new. It is easy out in nature to recount God's special personal blessings and to lift my heart in worship.

When it is necessary that I leave our mountain and drive alone down into the valley for doctor's appointments, shopping, or business, I often use travel time to worship, either in song or reciting Scripture aloud. Or sometimes I just pray aloud all the way, telling God how much I want to please Him in my lifestyle and ministry.

God has blessed me greatly through the ability to memorize Scripture. Sometimes He impresses me with special verses and chapters to memorize. Reciting them back to Him is one of my favorite ways to worship. In fact, I think He encourages me to memorize them for that very purpose!

Over the years I have collected verses that seem to draw my heart out to an ever deepening intimacy with God. I call them my "yearning" verses and keep them handy on index cards in my Bible case. Often, either at the beginning or the close of my morning prayertime, I read several of them back to God in worship, letting my heart long for more of the presence of God in my life. One of my favorites is Psalm 63:1-8:

> "O God, you are my God,
>   earnestly I seek you;
> my soul thirsts for you,
>   my body longs for you,
> in a dry and weary land
>   where there is no water.
> I have seen you in the sanctuary
>   and beheld your power and your glory.
> Because your love is better than life,
>   my lips will glorify you.
> I will praise you as long as I live,
>   and in your name I will lift up my hands.
> My soul will be satisfied as with the richest of foods;
>   with singing lips my mouth will praise you.
> On my bed I remember you;
>   I think of you through the watches of the night.
> Because you are my help,
>   I sing in the shadow of your wings.
> My soul clings to you;
>   your right hand upholds me."

Nothing has ever blessed me so much as my "yearning" verses. They seem to drive away indifference and raise the joy level in my heart, giving me a deeper sense of intimacy with God.

During the years when my husband pastored a church and we lived near other members, we often had several weeknight groups that met at our home to study, pray, and sing. Every Friday night a larger group met especially to worship in song. Anytime you can gather two or more Christians together is a wonderful opportunity to worship. I think it might be a good plan to suggest that your Sabbath school class take the first five minutes in worship and praise.

Well, there you have a few suggestions of ways to incorporate special worship times into your life. I am eagerly anticipating hearing from some of you the ways that God has led you to worship. God initiates all true prayer, praise, and worship. True worship in spirit and in truth must come from a worshiping heart in tune with God. Worship is our response of love to the love God felt for us before He created even the first human couple. Our expression of that worship not only pleases God, but makes the whole experience more real to us and thus leads to greater worship.

As I wrote this book I have often returned to edit, rewrite, and add to one particular chapter—chapter 3, on lifestyle worship. Unless our lives exhibit that we are walking in the Spirit, our verbal worship is worth little. Unless we treat our families, our neighbors, our fellow workers, with love and consideration, we might as well quit acts of outward worship, for they are meaningless. How we treat our children in the privacy of our homes, our patience (or impatience) with the clerk in the department store, the consideration we show other drivers on the freeway, our behavior in the line at the church potluck—all these reveal our inner relationship with God. Loving, abiding, and serving others sum up the kind of lifestyle worship acceptable to God.

Worship is not majestic organ music, trained voices, or stained-glass windows. It is hearts filled with adoration and reverent submission to God. If we have a daily relationship, an *alive and growing relationship with Jesus,* we will not just recite old words about it. We will be ever breaking out in entirely new words and ways to describe the joy of our ever-growing relationship!

What a privilege it is to worship God! He never turns a deaf ear to us, but treasures our worship and praise and writes it down in a book. I want to worship Him all the days of my life!

Summary

Since few changes in human behavior occur except by deliberate choice, we can enrich our lives by choosing to include worship experiences that will draw us into intimacy with God.

In the beginning God created humanity in His own image. His purpose now is to re-create us into creatures who can joyfully and intelligently enter into an eternal relationship with the angels and with God the Father, God the Son, and God the Holy Spirit. They want to be able to enjoy our fellowship.

The sanctuary illustration reveals special times that are appropriate for worship. The morning and evening sacrifices prefigure morning and evening worship in the home. Worship in the sanctuary on the Sabbath centered on the table of shewbread, signifying that it was a day to especially worship God through His living Word.

The annual Day of Atonement was a time of heart-searching and repentance. It prefigured the pre-Advent work of judgment Jesus is doing right now in the Most Holy Place. Since we live in a specific time set apart by God to worship Him in spirit and in truth, what an opportunity we have to enter into special times of worship!

Because we are preoccupied with earthly affairs or do not practice contemplation, we may miss God's special calls to worship. But as our relationship with God develops into greater intimacy, we will more and more hear His call and respond to it.

We can enrich our relationship with God by deliberately adding special moments of worship. Here are some suggestions:

Music, praise, and Scripture are the voices of worship.

Learning worship songs and singing them back to God is a rewarding way to worship. You can sing around the home, in the car, or at your place of work. Memorizing the words to the songs you choose to sing will add to your worship experience. You can also worship as you listen to CDs and tapes.

Another special music worship experience is to take the seven steps of sanctuary prayer and choose a song to sing for each step—singing through the sanctuary.

Ellen White suggests spending an hour each day contemplating the life of Christ, especially the Crucifixion. This makes a good worship exercise.

Reviewing scriptural accounts of worship encounters Bible characters had and joining into their worship will make the people of old live again in your mind and also renew your own worship.

Fasting for a 24-hour period can be a worship experience as you let go of the world through your fast and take hold of God through prayer. Other fasts include the "Daniel" fast, which involves eating only plain food, with no sweets or fats; and a fast from TV and secular reading for a specified length of time. We must enter into any fast with a humble heart and for the purpose of worshiping God, not in receiving commendation from either God or human beings. (Read Isaiah 58 for God's admonition about fasting.)

Taking special times to worship God outdoors in nature is a refreshing way to plan a worship experience.

Reciting back to God the praise portions He has influenced me to memorize is a powerful way to worship. I often like to renew my heart-longing for God through repeating back to Him what I call "yearning" verses. They express my deep desire for God. Nothing else can satisfy such longing except an intimate relationship with God. Repeating them to God renews my great desire for intimacy with Him.

Another rewarding way to worship is in small groups, singing, praising, praying, and studying the Word. Worshiping together has great power.

How to Implement Worship in Your Own Life

Worship is not majestic organ music, trained voices, or stained-glass windows. It is hearts filled with adoration and reverent submission to God. If we have a daily relationship, an alive and growing relationship with Jesus, we will not just recite pious phrases, but will ever be breaking out in entirely new expressions and ways to describe the joy of our ever-growing relationship!

EPILOGUE

Worship, Theme of Eternity

This book began with the Eternal Three in Eden, completing the creation of earth with its crowning achievement of a man and a woman. It is fitting that it close with the coronation of Christ as King of kings, the earth re-created in Edenic beauty, and the joy and worship of thousands of thousands of earth's inhabitants redeemed by the blood of the Lamb.

The hope of all those who have believed on Jesus as the Redeemer of the world down through the ages is that He will come again, just as He promised, and take us to be with Him forever. Paul, not only an apostle but also a great prophet, looked forward to the time when Christ will return and give the mighty trumpet call that wakes the righteous dead to everlasting life. Angels will transport both the resurrected saints and those faithful ones still alive, who have played a part in lighting up the whole earth with the glory of God in the final days, from this ravaged earth to Jesus in the clouds. Then the great entourage will ascend into heaven, where the righteous, as priests, will take part with Christ in the judgment of the wicked for a thousand years.

Christ's glory will destroy those still living who have stubbornly resisted God's rule to the bitter end. Satan and his angels will be left alone to restlessly wander a ruined earth.

At the close of the millennium the final judgment of the wicked will be complete. Jesus will lead a triumphant multitude back to earth. His feet touch the desolate earth, flattening a place for the New Jerusalem upon the very place God had originally chosen for the earthly headquarters of His chosen people. John the revelator describes this great event:

"I saw the Holy City, the new Jerusalem, coming down out of heaven from God, prepared as a bride beautifully dressed for her husband. And I heard a loud voice from the throne saying, 'Now the dwelling of God is with men, and he will live with them. They will be his people, and God himself will be with them and be their God'" (Rev. 21:2, 3).

Jesus will raise the wicked dead to life, and Satan will immediately marshall them together in the last great battle.

But high above the Holy City God's great throne will appear, and in the presence of the vast accumulated host—the saved in the city, the unrepentant sinners who have been raised to life and are gathered around the city, Satan and his wicked angels, the holy angels, and interested onlookers from other planets—Jesus will be crowned Lord of all. Satan's battle forces will watch against their will. God's law will be glorified and shown to be just and righteous. Sinners will acknowledge their guilt, and every knee will bow before that throne, confessing that "Jesus Christ is Lord to the glory of God the Father." God's just punishment will be meted out to Satan and his angels and those who followed him.

Then God will complete His "strange act" of eliminating sin and sinners from the universe, scouring the entire earth with a cleansing fire, leaving it clean and ready to renew.

This time we will see firsthand the act of creation! God will re-create our earth in Edenic beauty, and you and I will view it with our own eyes, not dependent upon Bible writers for our information. We aren't told how long God will take to complete His exciting task, but I can well imagine that it will be six days—giving us opportunity to savor every intimate part of creation. At sundown on the sixth day I can see Him gathering the saints around Himself and exclaiming, "Now we celebrate! Enjoy this special Sabbath, for it is just a taste of all the Sabbaths of the future. This glorious world is yours for eternity!"

What a time to worship! Although we experience wonderful times of worship now, and will enjoy worship face-to-face with God during the 1,000 years in heaven, worship in the re-created earth after the eradication of sin and the wiping away of all tears will be beyond anything we can imagine.

"And the years of eternity, as they roll, will bring richer and still more glorious revelations of God and of Christ. As knowledge is progressive, so will love, reverence, and happiness increase. The more men learn of God, the greater will be their admiration of His character. . . .

"The great controversy is ended. Sin and sinners are no more. The entire universe is clean. One pulse of harmony and gladness beats through the vast creation. From Him who created all, flow life and light and gladness, throughout the realms of illimitable space. From the minutest atom to the greatest world, all things, animate and inanimate, in their unshadowed beauty and perfect joy, declare that God is love" (*The Great Controversy*, p. 678).

I plan to be there. From one Sabbath to another, I plan to worship before the Lord. In fact, every day of my life, every moment, I want to worship Him. And you—will you be there too?

It is a privilege to learn to worship Him now, morning and evening, on the holy Sabbath hours, in special chosen moments, and also in our lifestyle, living only to glorify His name!